Published by Omphaloskepsis Press
a division of Mho and Mho Works

Additional copies may be ordered from the publisher:
  Mho and Mho Works
  Box 33135
  San Diego, Calif.
  92103
Price: $7.50 plus 50¢ postage and handling

———————————————————————————————

Also available from Mho and Mho Works:

The Merkin Papers (Duck Press)

Sex and Broadcasting (Dildo Press)

The Petition Against God (Christ the Light Works)

Coming soon from Mho and Mho works:
The Radio Papers (Mildewed Ear Press)

———————————————————————————————

Made in the U.S.A.

MASTURBATION, TANTRA and SELF LOVE

———

Margo Woods

Dedication

This book is dedicated
To John-David Schonbrook
And to Pluto and Pan
Three Great Crusaders for Positive Sexuality

Introduction

The word *Masturbation* comes to us from the latin "man(u)stuprare." Manu or Manus means "hand." Stuprum means "a dishonor, a defilement, a disgrace." Turbare, one of the etymological cousins of stuprum, means "to disturb, agitate, confuse." It is allied to the word stupid, and stupefaction. Now you see what we have to deal with.

The other day a friend and I sat around and tried to think of all the phrases we could come up with that mean to masturbate. We figured out a dozen or so. There's the "off" school: beating off, jacking off, jerking off, whacking off, whipping off, teeing off, ringing off. Then there are the intellectual ones: onanism, auto-eroticism, self-flagellation. There is too the opprobrious school (self-abuse, self-pollution, playing with yourself, tinkering, diddling, going to hell). Finally—the silly ones: Five Finger Freddy, doing your homework, whipping the snake, and my own personal favorite, a visit to "Rosie Palm and the Five Kidz." I'm sure you can think of others.

Back in the days of Bundles for Britain and Harry James, when Frank Sinatra was skinny and Doris Day sang "I Didn't Know What Time It was;" back when I was a tad just discovering the pleasures of the Lizard, that wonderful basket of fun down there—we, my friends and I, discussed our solitary accomplishments at great length. Scott, and Homer, and Tyler and I would compare figures for the quickest jerk-off, or the longest shot, or the suspected record for total beat offs in one day (I said eight, Tyler, an obvious consummate tale-teller, laid claim to an even dozen between sunrise and sunset).

Then Alfred Kinsey came along and blew the top off everything and put us all to shame. The book was *Sexual Behavior in the Human Male,* and it was published in 1948. I reread it recently and was amazed at the revolutionary style of the book. Kinsey truly laid to waste dozens of myths, and amidst all the charts and graphs, he wrote with a clarity and conviction that changed—once and for all—the attitude of Americans towards their own bodies and their own loves.

Kinsey taught us that we were not alone. We found out that thirty-five percent of all American males had sexual relationships with other males at some point in their lives. We found out that sixty-five percent of all females masturbate—and more frequently, as they get older. We found out that ninety-four percent of all males had masturbated at some time in their lives, and that the other six percent were obviously Baptist ministers who lied to save their necks. We found out that even at age fifty, over half the males are still masturbating during the course of a single week. And in keeping with Tyler's fishing tale about his own prodigeous sexual capacities, some respondents whacked off twenty-three times a week in early adolescence, and even at age fifty, a few hardy souls were putting in two dozen shots a month. A true eye opener.

Masturbation has been under attack for so long: the Bible has the famous interdicts against Self-Pollution, and we know the evil of Onan (who some of us, to be contrary, claim as our patron saint). The Boy Scout's Manual (up to twenty years ago), claimed that self-abuse would cause various bad things to happen. How far we have gone in so few years. If you were born in America up to twenty-five years ago, you would have been told (according to Kinsey's research) that masturbation would create ''every conceivable ill from pimples to insanity, including stooped shoulders, loss of weight, fatigue, insomnia, general weakness, neurasthenia, loss of manly vigor, weak eyes, digestive upsets, stomach ulcers, impotence, feeblemindedness, and genital cancer.''

From this you can guess why our ancestors were so feeble-minded on the subject of love—for (as Margo will point out to you later on) you cannot truly experience love without having experienced self love. That such a sweet cane box of pleasure should be lying so close at hand, and should be subjected to such vulgar attacks, makes us want to pity our grandmothers and grandfathers, those with such a desire to explore their own love-making apparatuses, yet believing that it would cause them to go blind or idiotic, or at best to grow luxuriant plantations of red hair on the palms of their hands. In those days, habitual masturbators, if caught, were punished or put in the funny farm. To keep their hands out of trouble they were placed in restraints and strait-jackets. As Kinsey points out, there was no way the medical doctors would admit that their own jerk-off rate was equal to the frequency of the loonies whom they salted away for these self-same, self-induced pleasures.

We all have our favorite masturbation stories, and favorite almost-got-caught stories. If we are brave enough, and have friends who are as enlightened and funny as we ourselves, we also have a chance to compare Method. One of my friends cannot make it with himself unless he is bare-assed naked on the carpet, with a sock on his cock. He reports that his mother once came into the bathroom and almost stepped on his bare butt. (That may or may not have been fantasy; the wonderful thing about masturbation stories is that they give us full range to our fantasy for, after all, who is there to check up and see if you are fibbing?)

My friend John uses his time alone in bed to play with all the parts of himself, twisting, pinching his own nipples, moving body and ass around everywhere on the bed. (I used to think that he was just being vulgar; now I think he may have found a secret for honorable self love).

Another of my friends is into Technique and Machinery. He uses ice cubes on his balls, claiming that they shrink up deliciously tight to his body, as they do on approaching orgasm. Another likes Dr. Bronner's Peppermint Soap for its spicy invigorating explosion of tang across belly and balls. Another runs a hair brush gently across the upper part of his legs or stomach or nuts. Another lets a single stream of water from the shower head run directly down on the neck of his penis: he says that the orgasm is involuntary and huge.

Self love is what it is, and that is what Margo has called this book. It is my feeling that all love should be self love, even plain, down-home fucking. I cannot spot the difference between the act of intercourse and the act of masturbation, except for the delicious presence of another person. And suppose you rub against your partner's thighs, or arms, or feet. Is that masturbation or fucking?

The difference we have created between the so-called Normal and the so-called Aberrant sexual behavior patterns is the sure sign of an aberrant attitude towards the whole beauty of love and bodies and the sexual experiment which is, after all, life and living. Men in this country (and in most of the western world) have been conditioned to think of sex as something you would plug into, like a wall socket. And, like a wall socket, it is harsh and buzzing and unnaturally cold.

We men pay the price for thinking of women as pieces of meat, as the road to the three minute shoot-off. Much of our violence flows from the hate we impose on ourselves, on our sexual partners, and on the imperfect children that must sprout from these imperfect unions. If there is nothing else to be learned from this book, it is that self love—without shame, with good humor, with a willingness to experiment—is the key to a healthy society and healthy relationships between men and women.

I have found almost no books on this important subject. In 1974 Betty Dodson published *Liberating Mastur-bation*. (It costs four dollars from Box 1933, New York City, 10001). In 1979 Manfred F. DeMartino edited *Human Auto-Erotic Practices,* a series of essays on the art of masturbation which ended with a wonderful list of objects found in nineteenth century England up the vaginas of lusty but incautious Victorian ladies: bottles, jars, hair pins, pokers, hair brush handles, and in one commodious farmer's wife, a whole duck egg. Their excuses, uniformly: ''I sat on it.''

None of these books expressed the marvelous message that Margo is giving us here, that is, love for the self can be translated into a means of achieving energy release, spiritual growth, and a method of plumbing new artistry in thinking, feeling, writing, and growing. It is an idea whose time has come.

Margo Woods' task in this book is to bring many of us out of the closet so that we can praise the pleasures of ourselves, rather than hide from them. What she has to tell us about love applies not only to women, but to all humanity. Loving yourself, without guilt, with—yes— dedication, and a sense of fun, is a special pleasure which does not have to be condemned as the solitary pursuit to keep the mental patient off the street, to keep the moron from impregnating his moron sister, to while away the long voyage of the sailor or assuage the businessman in some drab motel in Iowa City.

Rather, Margo's message, one that I hope you will

come to appreciate, is that most of us have deep love within us, waiting to be reached. As we do so, we are able to open new vistas of pleasure, insight, spiritual growty, ecstasy, and enlightenment. We ignore this path of warmth and liberation at our own loss.

A.W. Allworthy
Paradise, California
June, 1981

Preface

My purpose in writing this book is to show you how to love yourself and what you can expect to happen if you do.

My experiment began with a study of Tantra, the use of sexual energy to open the chakras. I was taught a certain technique, which is explained in this book, and then taught it myself for three years across the U.S. and Canada under the title of The Sexual Energy Seminar.

Most books on Tantra are either extremely esoteric, or extremely complicated. The esoteric ones promise ecstasy beyond our wildest dreams but tell us nothing about how to get there. The complicated ones give us breathing exercises, rules, and rituals, all of which take the spontaneity out of sex and require that you keep the book beside your bed in order to follow the proper sequence.

What these books lack is an alchemy, a method of producing the internal changes which result in expanded states and the opening of the chakras. It's an alchemy that is needed to open the heart and creates the love: self love or any other kind. For a civilization on the brink of disaster or enlightenment, nothing could be more useful than a system which opens the heart. And nothing could be more erroneous than thinking that love will solve all our problems. We need courage, good judgement, and creativity as well.

What is remarkable and useful about what I teach is that it is extremely simple, specific, and remarkably effective. It is an alchemy. No amount of rules and exercises can create passionate erotic responses. The sex chakra, the erotic nature, must be opened first. And passion is ephemeral, wasted, without knowledge of how to direct it, how to raise it upward in the body and use it to open the other centers.

This book is about becoming passionate and using passion to experience the divine. The method also has implications for healing, the creative process, relationships, and correction of sexual dysfunctions. It comes with warnings on the label, explained in chapter nine.

First of all, we must realize that we are suffering as a culture from some 2,000 years of our history in which sex has been thought of as evil and dirty. The historical picture is important, because we tend to think that whatever our cultural preferences are, is The Truth. However, with respect to sex we can see that there are many cultures prior to and emerging alongside the monotheistic Judeo-Christian one in which we were all raised, which not only had an easy and natural and wholesome attitude towards sex, but even some which saw it as one of the pathways to the divine.

I have had ample opportunity to observe the tragic results of these many years of repression of humankind's sexual impulses in my work as a traveling teacher and as a consultant at a sex therapy and sex education clinic. The clients at the clinic were otherwise normal people who came to see us because they couldn't have orgasms, couldn't allow themselves to have pleasure, couldn't relate to other people well enough to get a relationship going. Some suffered from the curses of modern manhood: premature ejaculation and impotence.

There is seldom any physical reason for these maladies, yet they are serious maladies. A man who is impotent cannot feel like a man. A woman who cannot have an orgasm cannot feel complete as a woman. This "human sexual inadequacy," as Masters and Johnson called it, affects all areas of their lives, and when the inadequacy disappears, the other areas of their lives—relationships, work, self confidence, physical appearance and attractiveness—change too.

Now with pioneers like Kinsey, the people who developed birth control, and Masters and Johnson, aided in no small measure by *Playboy* and other publications, sex is gradually creeping out of its wolves' clothing into its opposite, a natural and enjoyable human function and a pathway to the divine.

The Tantric technique has expanded into the concept of self love, a result of making love to oneself and of opening the heart. Self love becomes the basis of personal sanity and healthy romantic relationships.

I have experimented with this method for five years. It is my experience that sensuality and sexual energy, if used "as directed" are a means of expanding our consciousness, experiencing altered states, and improving the quality of our lives.

Margo Woods
San Diego, California
June, 1981

Masturbation, Tantra

Chapter One

The Barriers

Against Sexual Energy

The use of sexual energy to alter states of consciousness has not been popular for many centuries, if at all. We have dim reports from pre-Christian cultures and obscure Indian sects, but little is known about their actual practices and methods. We have had in our cultures, and not only Western cultures, strong taboos against sexuality, pleasure, and self love.

It begins at our birth. Almost all of us are born through the genitals of women who hated and feared their own sexuality. As they were growing up they gradually tightened their pelvic muscles against the flow of sexual energy, and when it came time to give birth to us it was very difficult for them to release those muscles and to let us pass through. Instead, our births were a struggle; we fought against the barriers imposed against our forward movement; and they, in pain, cursed us and the sexual impulses which put us inside there in the first place. According to Frederick Leboyer, author of *Birth Without Violence,* as we finally pass through the channel, we also cannot help but feel the disgust and fear they feel for that area of their bodies, and we absorb it into our own psyches.

Every time they change our diapers and look at that area of our bodies, more rejection and disgust are registered. As they wipe the shit from our bottoms we get the message very clearly that they don't like that area of our bodies, including the genitals, and we take on that disgust.

If we ever notice any pleasant sensations and respond to them with our hands, we are given the strictest threats against touching ourselves and following our natural pleasure.

Shortly afterward we are encouraged to stay clothed, segregated from members of the opposite sex when bathing, eliminating, and sleeping, and of course, we are told little or nothing about how our sexual energy works. Even though we may be told where babies come from, we are not told about passion.

By the time we are teenagers we are estranged from our bodies, our sexual energy, and from others who might have been our partners in joy and pleasure.

When we finally come together as couples we wonder why it all doesn't work very well—why there is so little sensuality, so little passion, and so many outright sexual dysfunctions, for example, men who come too fast and women who can't come fast enough. It puts a tremendous strain on our love for each other, since we cannot be satisfied in one of the primary functions of our being together.

I have worked with hundreds of people through the Sexual Energy Seminars, and as adults they have pretty much the same complaints:

Sex doesn't exist, or shouldn't exist.
Good sex is hard to come by.
I don't deserve good sex because my body isn't beautiful.
I don't attract anyone.
I'm afraid of sex.
I'm afraid of men.
I'm afraid of women.
I'm tired of having to perform in bed and put my partner first.
My body doesn't turn on very easily.
My body doesn't stay turned on.
All he/she wants me for is my body.
Sex is wrong, sinful, dirty.
God doesn't like sex.
If you're really spiritual you're celibate.
Sex isn't good for me.
Sex will get you into trouble.
You can catch diseases from sexual contact.
I can't find the right partner.
Nice girls don't.
If I get involved with someone sexually that means I owe them something.
I can't enjoy sex unless 1) I'm in love, 2) I'm not in love, 3) I'm drunk or stoned, 4) Fill in your own.

When we decide to heal ourselves we come up against some powerful forces. The first and most powerful is that our parents usually don't like sex and the belief is that if we heal ourselves and start enjoying our sexuality, then they won't like *us*. Most of us are little children inside, who still react to our parents as if we were two or three years old and dependent upon them for life and love. We believe that we can't survive their disapproval.

Secondly, as we look around us, we do not see very many people who have their sexual energy moving through their bodies in a joyous and healthy way. As I observe my fellow human beings in the supermarket and on the street, I do not find them very sexy. What would happen if I opened up my sexual energy? Would I go crazy? Would I be horny all the time? Would people reject and ostracize me, even punish me?

Nor is there help from the New Age spiritual community. Many members and groups in this community have even adoped the traditional position of celibacy as a superior spiritual position, thus reinforcing the cultural conditioning against their own sexual force. There is a truth in this position, but it is only a half truth. Since raising the level of consciousness requires raising the level of energy in the body, and since orgasm ordinarily lowers the level of energy (we usually roll over and fall asleep), then orgasm is seen as contrary to spiritual development, which depends on raising the level of energy in the body. So the easiest way to avoid orgasm is to avoid sex altogether. (This theory will be explained in chapter eight.)

What I recommend to my students will be discussed in the next chapter. It actually works against the three problem areas I have just mentioned. First, working with the sexual energy in this way helps the inner child to grow up and to have more strength to break the parent-induced patterns. It also gives him/her a sense of confidence, centering, and personal identity which are necessary to become a whole person. Nancy Friday, in *My Mother, Myself,* stresses that a strong sexual identity and connection to one's sexuality is necessary to break the negative conditioning from our parents.

Secondly, my experience with opening the sexual energy in myself and others is that it is not a handicap in relating to other people, but rather an asset. I have become more loving and more powerful and more attractive. I have not been rejected on account of my heightened sexuality, nor am I crazed or horny all the time.

The solution to the spiritual question is to substitute the whole truth for the half truth. If you delay your orgasm and raise the energy up in your body, you will eventually reach a level of energy at which orgasm does not bring you down. And in the meantime you will benefit from the effects of that energy flowing through your body whether you have orgasms at the end of your sessions or not.

The Sexual Revolution has begun. Everyone, or almost everyone, knows it's OK to be sexual. Why aren't we having more fun? Why doesn't it all work? The answer is that it doesn't work because we have, like good children, shut off our sexuality, our erotic nature.

So now that we have seen how we have lost the beauty and power of our passionate nature, let's find out how to get it back. Human beings are sexual and passionate by nature, and it is not difficult to remove the negative conditioning and allow the natural human being to replace the conditioned one.

Chapter Two

The Road Back Home

I have been on a concentrated program to discover the nature and uses of my sexual energy for the last nine years. I first heard the word *Tantra* in London in 1971. I was visiting an artist friend who insisted that I go to see an exhibit of Tantric art. I was fascinated. Here were some ancient people who had said that sexual energy was not only beautiful and valuable, but a way to experience God!

Meanwhile, my own sex life was very tame. I had just read Dr. Ruben's book, *What You Always Wanted to Know About Sex,* and thanks to his graphic description of an orgasm, I realized that I had never had one. Although I loved sex, and it was always very magical to me, I wasn't even making it to first base. So I did as he recommended, bought a vibrator, and made the great discovery. But it wasn't until I came to San Diego in 1974 that I started making some huge leaps in my sexuality. In San Diego I worked with two sex therapists who taught me first to masturbate and then to satisfy myself with a partner.

A year later I met a man who introduced himself as a Tantra Master and agreed to teach me. His main teaching was the one I give my students in the Sexual Energy Seminars. His instruction to me was to make love to myself, to masturbate, and to stop at the point just before orgasm, put my attention in my heart, and let the energy go up to my heart. The exact point to stop, he said, was the point where you know that one more stroke will make you come. "Just take your hand away," he said, "and let the energy go up to your heart." After each rush of energy to the heart I was to resume masturbating, repeating the cycle, until there seemed to be no more energy, or I felt like stopping. There was no prohibition against orgasm, only the requirement to delay it, letting the energy go to the heart first. Delaying my orgasms in this manner, I found, made them more intense.

He told me to do the exercise every day for three months. I did, and it has been a part of my life ever since. This simple exercise has proven to be a method of internal alchemy, a method by which I have begun to make changes in my psycho-physical system and thus changes in my states of consciousness.

After a year of being with him and practicing the exercise over and over, I had two classical, out-of-the-book experiences in altered states, one with a partner and one by myself. In the first instance, I went to a friend's birthday party and wound up going home with a man I met there. We went to bed that Saturday night and didn't get up except to eat and pee for almost seventy-two hours. During most of that time we were engaged sexually in a state of unity with each other and the cosmos, a non-verbal state in which we didn't know who had which body or what our names were. He stayed hard the entire time, and we lost track of the number of orgasms. We broke the experience because we started to wonder what the rest of the world must be doing, and we got up to have a look. We stayed very psychically connected to each other for days, knowing each other's thoughts and whereabouts, but we never got together again. I took it as a gift from the universe, a show of the possibilities.

Another gift came in a session I had by myself. I was doing the Fischer-Hoffman Process, an intense three month therapy, and had been working with a spiritual guide as part of the process, meditating and talking to him every day. He only came into my thoughts when I called on him. On this particular day I was doing the masturbation exercise and got very horny. In fact I was thinking of someone I could call and ask to come over and play. All of a sudden my guide interrupted my thoughts and said sharply, "Now you listen to me. I want you to understand that you don't need *anyone* to make this energy work for you, and I'm going to prove it to you. You just keep doing your exercise and I'll show you that you can get higher than you ever believed possible."

So I kept on doing the exercise, running the energy up to my heart. After awhile I decided to come, which would ordinarily lower the level of energy and end the session. However, this time it didn't seem to. I suspected that I had reached a level of energy which I had only heard about, where orgasm doesn't bring you down. I decided to test it, and I came again and again, each time after a few rounds of bringing the energy up to my heart. An hour and a half and eighteen orgasms later, I simply stopped out of boredom and went to take a walk on the beach. At that time I did not think of myself as a very attractive woman, but on this particular day people turned their heads as I walked on the sand. I felt like a goddess and I must have been glowing.

My relationship with the teacher had ended before I had these experiences, but I felt that they gave me the authority to begin teaching others what I knew. I decided that my progress was due not only to my training with him, but also because I had been doing so much emotional release work and meditation that my system was more open and clearer than most. I decided to include release work and meditation and a lot of clearing of negative sexual conditioning in my workshop. As I progressed with the workshop and continued the exercise myself, I became more and more amazed at the value of the technique. About six months after I started teaching the workshop I met another man with whom, after a couple of sessions together, I had a classical heart opening experience. What I mean by that is, the experience of being in love but without another person to be in love with, "Pure Love," as described in the chapter on theory. In other words, I was in love with everyone and everything, felt totally at peace and physically beautiful. I was loving and clear and loved. I became Love Itself. The experience lasted for several days.

More important than the experience of an altered state in these few days was the fact that my heart was clearly opening bit by bit. I became more loving, and more able to express love to others, more patient, more open, and less afraid of other people or their disapproval. I began to see my heart as a psychic organ as well as a physical one. I could put my attention in my heart when talking to a friend or client and know, in some inexplicable way, what they needed from me and how to give it to them.

Then in Montreal things began to pop. Two participants in the workshop had classical experiences in higher states of consciousness while doing the exercise, on their first try! I was elated. And the reports kept coming in from workshop graduates all over the country: "I no longer have any trouble attracting loving sexual partners." "I no longer have a problem with premature ejaculation." "Sex just gets better and better." I could see that the experiences I had were not individual and peculiar to myself, but could be experienced by anyone, either immediately or over a period of time.

I, too, along with my students, became more magnetic and more satisfied with the ease and pleasure of my sexual experiences. It seems that the most important ingredient of sexuality is that personal magnetism, that magnetic attraction. With it, sex is easy. Without it, sex becomes a hassle and a chore. The masturbation exercise, without a doubt, increases one's personal magnetism.

I also began to see that my vitality, my aliveness, and my enthusiasm were increasing noticably. Friends remarked how wonderful I looked, how alive I was. I began to learn that I could direct the energy to any part of my body, not only my heart, and began using it for healing, directing it to any place in my body that wasn't feeling right. I am now directing it to my third eye (an energy center in the forehead) and my *hara* (an energy center in the belly) and am finding that my mind is clearer and I have more courage and a sense of personal power I didn't have before.

The effects have been especially dramatic with respect to the third eye. I was having trouble writing this book: in fact, I wasn't writing anything, but I was suffering a lot over it. Finally, on the way to do a workshop in Hawaii in January of 1979, the airlines lost my suitcase, and along with it, my manuscript.

I spent a couple of days being completely at a loss, and then remembered having read somewhere that sexual energy could be used for creative work and problem solving. I decided that it must be that one would flood the body with energy, using my self love technique, aiming the energy at the third eye and not coming, so as to keep all the energy available in the body.

So I had a session with myself and sat down to my typewriter. To my surprise, I wrote the introduction and the first chapter in an hour and a half. The words flowed through me and into the typewriter like magic writing. I was amazed. The first four chapters were written in my two week stay in Maui, and the rest came together with remarkable swiftness.

Shortly after I returned to the mainland, I was asked to write a column on sexuality for a newspaper which was just putting out its premier issue. I had never done such a thing before, but decided to try, using my new-found method for stimulating my creativity. It was the easiest thing I've ever done. I turned out a bi-weekly column for eight months and never was at a loss for ideas. I received a letter from the editor and publisher towards the middle of that time, stating that the column was being received with the highest praise by readers and was one of the chief contributions to the success of the paper.

And the writing has expanded further. It seems that a creative process has been stimulated which I no longer have to prod with any methods whatsoever. Almost every week I'll have an idea for an article to write for a magazine, a short story, or a poem. I am turning into a prolific writer! I have no doubt but that it is a result of stimulating my third eye with vital energy. The process should work the same for artists, musicians, and businessmen with problems to solve.

There is a word of caution here. I was told by my teacher, and I tell my students, to work with the heart center first. For one thing, you will probably not be able to generate enough energy to make it all the way to the head at first, but the most important thing is that the heart is a great safety valve. If the heart is open, even a little, there is no tendency to hurt oneself or others. Love wishes everyone well. The problem that I see with many people who are taking this spiritual path is that they try to work on the upper centers before they work with the body and the heart. These are the ''bliss ninnies'' who can't seem to function on what they call ''the material plane,'' and have a strong tendency towards paranoia because their bodies are unbalanced and their hearts are closed. A person with a closed heart is afraid of other people.

Work on your heart first. When you start to feel yourself loving the people in the supermarket and crying at parades you will probably be ready to work on the other centers.

One of the most interesting aspects of this process has been that my students and I have developed an unshakable sense of identity and OKness about ourselves. This is the self love which is talked about so much in books and workshops these days. Have you ever asked, "How?" when the workshop leader said that it is important to love yourself? This way of using the sexual energy produces self love more intensely than any other exercise I have ever tried. *One learns to love oneself by making love to oneself.*

One of the greatest compliments ever given to me by a workshop participant came after the San Francisco workshop in February of 1979. A man in his thirties stood up at the end of the workshop and said, "You know, I've been to a lot of workshops in the last five years, taught by some of the biggest names in the growth movement, and I've heard over and over again that what we all need is to learn to love ourselves. But I never had anyone who could show me how to do it until now. Thank you."

I want to give you enough in this book that you can duplicate all of the experiences of myself and my students and learn for yourself how simple and easy and joyful sex can be.

First of all, accept the fact that you were trained out of your sexuality from an early age. Go over the list of negative positions and statements in the last chapter. How many are yours? What others are yours? What negative thoughts go through your mind when you think about masturbation or sex with a partner, or any other aspect of the game? When you're in bed with someone, where does the energy break down?

Begin talking back to yourself when these negative thoughts come up, for example, "I know my mind is telling me that sex is a hassle and I'd rather not bother with it. But I know now that this is a result of my conditioning and I am going to work against it by doing the masturbation exercise and putting myself in situations where a sexual experience may occur."

Next, take off your clothes and look at yourself in a full length mirror. Ask yourself what parts of your body you like and what you don't like. Realize that what you don't like is not only conditioned by a *Playboy/Playgirl* image of what is beautiful, but is one of the many ways you keep your body frozen and incapable of transmitting sexual energy. In so far as you don't like your body, you freeze your sexual energy. Realize also that you can change your body if you want to, with diet, exercise, and wardrobe changes. If you can't love your body the way it is, then change it.

Take long baths, relaxing and washing yourself tenderly with your bare hands. Give extra attention to the parts of your body you don't like, massaging them gently and lovingly and apologizing to them for not loving them more. If you like oils on your skin, be conscious and slow while you massage them on to your skin, again giving extra care and attention to the parts which need more love. Participate in any activity or class which will make your body feel good to you.

As for the masturbation exercise, the only thing to remember is that it is extremely simple—raising the body's sexual energy almost to the point of orgasm, and instead of letting the energy go out into the orgasm, allow it to come up in the body, up to the heart. It happens that, at the point just before orgasm, there is a channel open in the body, and if you rest at that point and put your attention in your heart, the energy which has been generated will flow naturally upwards toward the heart. You don't have to *do* anything; it just happens. Don't worry about what it feels like, or if it is happening, just do it! Begin an adventure with yourself to see what your sexual energy is all about. Rediscover the physical system you were trained to ignore.

If you have difficulty talking yourself into a masturbation session, or in making love to yourself regularly, remember that you are conditioned away from that activity. Take the position that masturbation is now your meditation. Start your session by touching and loving yourself with your hands or soft fabrics all over your body before you go for your genitals and other erotic zones.

You may have an orgasm at the end of a session if you like, or you may find that you come by accident, and that will probably end your session for you because the energy will be gone. Men particularly will need to stop each round far short of orgasm till they learn what the point of no return is for them. Men will also discover that delaying orgasm or eliminating it altogether does not necessarily produce unpleasant sensations in the testicles. I have had enough men tell me this from their own experience that I now believe that the idea that a man *must* have orgasm or risk physical pain is erroneous. It certainly does not happen to men who are moving the energy upwards.

Many of my women students have eliminated menstrual cramps by masturbating and moving the sexual energy upwards. It seems that menstrual cramps are a result of sexual tension. Certainly the greatest sufferers from cramps are teenage girls, who have less outlet for their sexual impulses than adult or married women.

Other problems connected with repressed sexuality are bedwetting, acne, and diseases associated with sexual expression: the clap, vaginal fungus irritations, and so on. In Greece and Rome, and in the Far East before Christianity came, there was no VD. VD first appeared with Christianity, with guilt about sex, with trying to shove those powerful impulses out of sight. It is my opinion that all of the above symptoms are caused by repressed or conflicted sexuality. The repressed sexual energy has to go somewhere, and it come out in skin eruptions, genital diseases, and bedwetting.

The biggest problem you will have with this exercise is not how to do it, because it is extremely simple, but your own training against masturbation. A 1979 issue of *Playboy* contained an article which talked about the origin of our sexual hangups and showed that as a culture we have been conditioned not only out of sex, but out of *pleasure*. And self pleasuring, or masturbation, is the most forbidden pleasure of all. Examine your fears and feelings about masturbation. Then put them aside, and relearn your own body. *The pleasure you experience will do more to work against your negative conditioning about your body and your sexuality than anything else you can do or think.* I suggest you do what my teacher advised me to do—have a session with yourself every day, as a meditation, for three months, and see what the results are for yourself.

It is necessary to include a word about sexual fantasies. I can't imagine making love to myself without fantasies. They seem to create the experience for me. I suspect that much of the problem and lack of enjoyment people have with masturbation, in addition to their belief that it is wrong, is that they do not use their fantasies. All of us have a potentially rich fantasy life, a secret garden, as Nancy Friday calls it, which could enhance our sex lives immeasurably if we would let it. So go with your fantasies.   They won't hurt you—not even the weird ones.

I consider myself an explorer and adventurer in a territory which is available to everyone, but which is new because it has been closed to us for so long. Discovering myself has been a precious gift. I am delighted to pass the gift along to you.

Chapter Three

Being With A Partner

The most important thing to know about being with a partner is knowing how to be with yourself. It is absolutely necessary to have a private sex life in order to have a satisfactory sex life with a partner. For one thing, you need to have exact knowledge of how the energy works in your own body, and it is very difficult to learn this with another person to take into account at the same time. Sex therapy teaches people to masturbate, to learn their own bodies.

Secondly, making love with oneself successfully, learning that we can achieve ecstasy alone as well as with a partner, is a very powerful discovery. Most of us are waiting around for prince or princess charming to come and kiss us on the lips and wake us from our emotional and physical slumbers into the vital, passionate beings we know we truly are. Unfortunately it doesn't work that way. We become passionate beings by turning *ourselves* on, by opening our sexuality ourselves, by reversing the conditioning that closed it all off in the first place. And then when our energy is flowing, when we know how our own bodies work, we are ready for a partner.

The Eagles have a beautiful line in one of their songs that goes, *"I found out a long time ago what a woman can do for your soul, but a woman can't take you any place you don't already know how to go."* There may have been a very special night when you were carried into ecstasy with a very special partner, but those occasions will remain rare and isolated unless you individually do the work of opening your own sexuality.

I know this is true because I used to try to teach someone by going to bed with him. He, of course, having the expectation that I, the teacher, will be able to take him to those spaces he longs for. My universal experience in these situations is that *I* go to those spaces and he just has a wonderful sexual experience. In the Hindu tradition, even though the woman was regarded as the priestess, or the keeper of the secret, the male initiate had to train for years before he was considered ready to meet with one of those marvelous beings.

The value of all this in terms of the *relationship* between you and your lover is immense. If I don't depend on my lover for my highs, or blame him for my lows, then I can enjoy him when we come together and there is a loving lightness in our relationship that is very rich. I also don't have to be afraid of losing him, because 1) it's so good he'd be a fool to leave, and 2) if he does leave, I'm so attractive and magnetic and *satisfied with my life* that it's only a matter of time before another partner will appear.

Lastly, if we have opened our hearts to each other, which is possible when we raise the sexual energy to our hearts, then there is a bond formed between us, a pleasure bond. This bond will last through the times when our hearts may be closed, or we can't cope with the other aspects of our lives, and the times when the relationship appears not to be working.

With that introduction, let's talk about being together and using the sexual energy together to alter our states of consciousness. The secret of being with a partner is the same as the secret of being with oneself: to raise the energy in your body to the point of orgasm and then, instead of coming, relaxing and letting the energy go up to your heart. In other words, *there are no rules:* no special breathing, no positions, no sequence of events, no time allotments. Throw away your Tantra books! Throw away your sex manuals! Just bring the energy up to the point of orgasm, relax, and let it go up in the body instead of out into orgasm. You don't have to be at the brink together, either. I prefer to masturbate or be masturbated during lovemaking because it keeps the energy up very high, but *there are no rules.* You don't need any rules, because once the energy is flowing it will take you without a plan and you won't need a map. The discoveries I have made are largely due to the fact that I made few assumptions about where I was going.

If you find it difficult to delay your orgasm when you are with a partner, try stopping *several* strokes before orgasm and just relaxing, without doing anything else.

When you have accomplished simply *delaying* the orgasm, then try focusing on your heart and letting the energy come up.

Just as in your private sessions, you can repeat the cycle of stimulation and rest as often as you like and have an orgasm, if you wish, when you think your session is about over. Being finished is subjective. You're finished when you think you are. You should also experiment with not coming at all, just to break the belief that it is harmful or unsatisfying not to come.

I have counseled a number of couples regarding their sexual patterns and I find they are most concerned with those times when the sexual energy seems to shut down or won't get started at all. I suggest to them that if they will take an attitude of *play* towards their sex with partners (and of course with themselves as well) that they will feel satisfied and successful with their experiences more often. Having as a goal mutual orgasm, or the level of excitement you had last January when you were stoned on acid and had been meditating for four hours, is a setup for disappointment. Sometimes the body just isn't interested or the spirit is too burdened with other things. In the latter case, what often happens is that if the couple will just relax and be together, holding each other and chatting in a loving way, the emotional upsets will be discussed and cried about, and the couple will be able to make love when the tension is released. In addition, just lying around together nude and touching in a loving and non-goal oriented manner is a great way to get turned on. It's as if the body remembers, "Oh yeah, I *like* this stuff."

If you take an attitude of play, your lovemaking sessions will probably last longer, too, and you will find that in the course of each hour you are together that the intensity of the energy will rise and fall. Sometimes you'll be hot and sometimes you'll be sensual, and sometimes you'll just be friendly. We have a tendency to think that if it's not hot and heavy all the time there's something wrong. Usually if you just resume the attitude of loving play, the wave will return.

And what of the case in which the energy suddenly drops away to nothing when you are in the middle of a wave? Usually one or both partners has had a negative thought. "My body is ugly," or "He'll never give me what I want," or the sub-verbal messages that this great experience is somehow going to land us in hell and other difficulties. Here the remedy is the same: just lie around together and wait for the wave to come back. If you can remember the negative thought and can talk about it, some of its power will be defused.

I also encourage couples to go with their fantasies. Most people have a rich fantasy life, as mentioned before, but are unwilling to share it with their partners because they are afraid there's something wrong with them or that the partner will be offended. Couples who open their fantasy lives to each other find that it enhances their attraction to each other and the intensity of their sexual experiences, because together they devise all sorts of delightful sexual pastimes.

In addition, I teach in the workshop a number of games a couple can play which will probably raise the level of energy between them and make the journey more interesting. One such game is simply to breathe together. Just breathing at the same rate while you are holding each other can be ecstatic. Another is looking into each others' eyes. When I look into the eyes of another person for a long period of time, my thoughts stop, and I start to feel heat in my belly spreading throughout my body. But this is after years of practice. In the beginning you will experience some discomfort in looking into each others' eyes and will need to try it for only short periods of time. You will sometimes change the flavor of your meeting from a sexual one to an emotional one, but you can always go back to sex. Use the left eye; it's the receptive eye and connects to the right side of the brain.

Another delightful possibility is to bring sound into your sessions together. Try anything from chanting together to making unplanned, miscellaneous sounds together which will gradually take on a life of their own. There is something about making sounds together, vibrating together, which, like breathing together, makes us ecstatic. When I do this with a lover I feel like we become one, that our vibration somehow becomes one and I can feel the inside of his body as well as mine.

It also helps to practice being receptive. Most people have much more difficulty letting love and energy *into* their systems than letting it out, or being loving. So with your lover take turns playing parent and child as an exercise in learning to be receptive. The partner who plays the parent lies on their back and the partner who takes the position of child lies with their head on or near the parent's heart. The parent embraces the child, stroking them occasionally and imagining limitless love pouring from their heart into the child. Breathing together, the child just soaks it up (and watches what conflicts it produces for them). Then you switch.

I also like to play with visualizations and mantras. One visualization is to breathe together and imagine that the energy moves between you in a circle, going up the genitals of one partner, then across from their heart to the other's heart, down to that person's genitals, and around again. It can go either direction. This exercise is extremely important for the experience of unity and bonding which we seek with those we love. It is called "The Girdle of Venus," and produces intense effects over a period of time.

I also use mantram. A mantram is a sound or a phrase which is repeated over and over, either internally or aloud. The purpose of mantram, as I see it, is to help quiet the chatter in our heads so energy can move. The mantras I like are "Shiva, Shakti," "You love me," "We are one," and "I worship the god/goddess within you." The "Shiva, Shakti" seems to call the archetypal male/female energies into love making. "You love me" seems to create a circuit of energy between partners. "We are one" reminds us of our oneness, whether we experience it or not. "I worship the god or goddess within you" reminds me of who my partner really is and who I really am. I usually do the mantrams silently, in my head, and my partner may do them or not, as he pleases.

Another interesting connection is through the solar plexus. (To locate your solar plexus, run your fingers down your breastbone until it ends. Push your fingers into the hole there. This is where your solar plexus is. Focus on this point for this exercise). If we imagine that we are projecting a beam of light at each other, from each solar plexus across to the other, and breathe together, a wonderful connection happens. Likewise if we touch each others' solar plexuses and breathe together.

Any of the books you find on Tantra or the joys of sex may have games to play that will make your sexual experiences deeper and take you closer to the experience of unity. You don't need any of the exercises really; let your imagination and your love for each other inspire your sexual acivities.

Just remember there are no rules except getting the energy as high as possible and resting and allowing it to come up in the body. Go with the energy, go with your fantasies, go with the movements your body wants to make, and spend time alone sexually as well as with your partners. Eventually you will have the experiences you seek and then will have them with greater and greater regularity.

Sex is play. You begin to win in your sex life when you come from this position.

Chapter Four

Masturbation and Self Love

There are always a certain number of people who, when you tell them to masturbate, don't know what you're talking about, and others to whom masturbation means jacking off. This chapter is for them.

Masturbation is a dirty word in our culture—even dirtier than sex—and is done hurriedly in dirty, ugly places, like bathrooms. In fact, I've all but stopped using the word masturbation, because it really doesn't describe what I do in my sessions with myself, and I have begun substituting the words *self love,* or making love to myself.

I have been reluctant in the past to describe my personal sessions, not only from a sense of privacy, but because I stress to my students that there is no sexual method other than allowing the energy to move up in the body, and I was afraid that my students would copy my personal style rather than developing their own. However, having discovered the dismal state of the art of self love and the difficulties my students were having with it, I have at last included a chapter on ''how to do it'', or at least, how *I* do it. *Please* do not take this as a formula to be followed but only a stimulus for your own imagination and creativity.

Many of my personal sessions are short and to the point, working very quickly to the level of energy just before orgasm and running the energy up to my heart or another area of the body as many times and as rapidly as I can until the energy seems to be gone, or I am bored, or I come by accident or on purpose. These sessions last twenty minutes to one half hour and are like quickie meditations.

For beginners in masturbation, describing a longer session is more useful because they will need a longer time to turn themselves on, and get to the orgasm-is-imminent level.

First of all, think about what turns you on. Romantic or rock music? Candles and incense? Porno magazines? Satin sheets, fur rugs, fireplaces? Moonlight, waves crashing on the sand, warm, moist air on your skin? Dressing up in sexy underwear or tight jeans? Fantasies? Dildoes? Use them. Use all of them in whatever combination you like. Create for yourself in your bedroom or elsewhere an erotic environment using as many of your turn-ons and beautiful objects as you can.

You will do well to begin your sessions by relaxing your body in various ways, because we are all over stressed, and psychological stress and muscular tension interfere with the flow of energy in the body.

I like to take long hot baths or sit in a warm hot tub, surrounded by candlelight, incense, flowers, moonlight, consciously letting as many muscles relax as I can. I wash myself slowly and lovingly with my bare hands, conscious that my hands are connected to my heart and carry the impulse of love to whatever I touch. I give extra loving attention to the parts of my body I don't like much, like my belly and my thighs, and a little stimulus to my erogenous zones.

After one half to one hour in the bathtub I dry myself and massage my whole body with massage oil. I use vegetable oils like almond oil or apricot kernal oil from the health food store, with a little of my favorite perfume added. I discovered once, when I needed a massage and couldn't afford one, that I could massage my whole body myself, with the exception of a very small area of my back. Shoulders, neck, lower back, butt, as well as arms and legs and head, are easy to reach and knead out the tensions of the day.

After I finish going over my body in a therapeutic way, I begin again to go over my whole body in a sensual and tender way, caressing my face, my neck, my torso, being with myself first with a feeling of sensuousness and tenderness rather than eroticism. I include tenderness towards my erotic zones, but I don't focus on them. I fantasize, I may dress or partially dress erotically. I bring in my music or my magazines, or whatever I am attracted to for that day. I may caress my body with soft fabrics or feathers, or other textured things.

When I am feeling sensuous and ready I begin to stimulate my genitals and nipples and other turn-on spots, and gradually work the energy up towards that point just before orgasm that I want to use as my meditation.

For women who are unfamiliar with masturbation it is necessary to find the proper stimulation of nipples and clitoris, and it is necessary to keep the finger which works the clitoris moist. The easiest way to do this is to return it to the vagina frequently because there is usually a supply of just the right kind of moisture there. Saliva works fine, or a little oil can be kept close by in a bowl or convenient container so that the rhythm won't be broken by unscrewing caps and pouring. If you are having trouble finding your magic spot, try the upper part of the clitoral shaft, up towards the pubic bone, and the sides, rather than the end of it, or the ''head.''

I find that when I have stimulated myself close to orgasm I have considerable sensation in my vagina and around the vaginal lips, and fingers or a dildo at this time increase the total sensations dramatically. Find the spots *inside* which please you as well as outside, and learn to use them along *with* other forms of stimulation such as clitoral.

Once you have explored the inside of your vagina and discovered how soft and warm and luscious it is, and what turns you on there, you can also develop a stroking technique which is very pleasurable to you and to a cock, if it happens to be inside you. Try it with your fingers inside first so you can feel the loving stroking sensations yourself. First contract the pubo-coccygeus muscle and then push out, as if you were expelling something from the vagina. Get a comfortable rhythm going, contracting, pushing out, contracting, pushing out. The internal effect is a delicious kind of stroking or milking of whatever object is inside to receive it.

If you are not familiar with the pubo-coccygeus, or P.C. muscle (and both men and women should know how to use it), now is the time to learn. The P.C. muscle covers the entire pelvic floor, from the pubic bone in front to the tailbone in the back, and is spread out like a cradle from side to side. All the openings out of the lower part of the body go through this muscle. It has been known for centuries in the East (though only recently in the West) to be associated with sexual and vital energy. If this muscle is strong and in good tone both men and women find it easier to get turned on. Contracting the muscle as an exercise increases its tonus, and contracting it during lovemaking or masturbation increases the level of sexual stimulation and pleasure for both partners.

To learn how to use it, stop the flow of urine several times while you are urinating. The muscle you need to do this action is the P.C. muscle. Practice until it is easy for you to squeeze it strongly and repeatedly during your sessions. For women, put a finger inside the vagina to test how tightly you can grasp it. Men can test it by putting a finger inside the rectum.

When I first began my self love sessions I was already familiar with the P.C. muscle from my sex therapy and would squeeze it repeatedly as I was building up towards orgasm. Later on I thought I'd rather have less tension there and more relaxation, so I discovered that I could get the same effect by working my thigh muscles, which also connect up in the pelvis and go through the P.C. muscle. I kneel down with my thighs and calves at right angles to each other and lean back slightly as I am working my clitoris, and that increases the stimulation for me considerably.

Men are probably more familiar with masturbation than women, but directed towards getting off, and not towards self love. For men especially it is important to touch and make love to the whole body, not just the cock, to be sensual with oneself, not just beat off. Men who are not familiar with the sensations in their nipples and rectum should experiment with these also, thereby expanding their possibilities for sensation.

For the more adventuresome, both men and women, the rectum is also an erotic zone and a very powerful one. Unfortunately it is the most taboo area of the body and you may have to explore it slowly in order to overcome your prejudices. If you are worried about cleanliness, do a brief enema before beginning your explorations. We have the gay community to thank for opening up this avenue of eroticism.

The object of the whole meditation, of course, is to allow the energy to run up in the body as many times as you can. A daily session is recommended if you want to achieve the result of opening your chakras or energy centers. You are bombarding the heart from the inside with vital energy in order to stimulate it, so the more the better. However, I usually find that twenty to forty-five minutes of such stimulation is all my body wants. Sometimes the energy seems to run out, as if there was a daily supply which now has been moved upward, and sometimes I come by accident. In any case, the session will end of its own accord sooner or later. I still have a session almost every day.

Some people ask how I can stand being that close to orgasm and not coming. At first, I admit, it was a kind of exquisite torture. I had to promise myself before I started that I would raise the energy five or six times before coming and reward myself with an orgasm after that many cycles. But now there's no torture at all, and running the energy upward is *significantly more pleasurable than orgasm itself.* At present I have little interest in orgasm, but nothing against it. Orgasm ends the play, usually, so it should never be the only goal of a sexual experience.

People also ask what I mean by "putting your attention in your heart and allowing the energy to go there." If you don't know what putting your attention in your heart means, try first putting your attention in your finger. Hold up your index finger and look at it. Now feel that finger from inside. You will notice that there is a continuous sensation there, all you have to do is pay attention to it. Likewise, you can focus your attention in the area of your chest around your heart and you will notice sensations there too. Sometimes if you are relaxed and quiet enough, you can also feel it beating. Just put your attention in that area of your chest, as you did with your finger. As I explained before, the energy will naturally flow upward to that point, you don't have to do anything else. The same principle applies if you want the energy to go elsewhere in the body than the heart. Just stop short of orgasm and put your attention in the area of the body to which you want it to go.

Sometimes I have my sessions in the morning when I wake up, sometimes at night before I go to sleep, or before I am to be with a lover, and sometimes during the day when I need a lift, psychologically or physically. It was several years of masturbating before I discovered that what it should be about is self love. I hope these suggestions will help you over some of your fears and confusion about msturbation and give you the courage to discover the value of making love to yourself.

Chapter Five

How to Find
Your Soul Mate

I grew up, as do most Americans, with the fantasy that some day my prince would come, and this prince charming would carry me off on his white horse and we'd live happily ever after. When I met him, we got married, but we didn't live happily ever after, and eight years and two children later, in a total state of disillusionment, we were divorced.

‹ In recent years I have been nagged by the suspicion that perhaps, just perhaps, Prince Charming doesn't exist—that there are only ordinary men out there with problems of body and soul just like mine—and no one who is going to scoop me up on his white horse and take me off to his castle for evermore.

I've been watching my women friends, and my men friends too, and no one seems to be faring much better than I. Of course there are times when we *think* we've found *the one* and for weeks, or sometimes even months, we sail through our lives in a state of bliss, but we always come down, and look back on the affairs with a sense of bewilderment. "how could I ever have been in love with *him?* (or *her*)."

Nevertheless the notion of a special person, a forever person, a soul mate, persists. No matter how much my rational mind tells me that he doesn't exist, my irrational mind insists that he is just around the corner, just out of sight.

There is a growing literature in the New Age movement which talks about Soul Mates—how to find them, what to do after you find them, how to know if this is really the one, and so on. Popular literature, movies, and ballads still present the basic story of Cinderella and Prince Charming, despite increasing sophistication in other matters. In fact, the theory of soul mates sounds a lot like a space-age Cinderella story.

Three or four years ago, when I had been living in San Diego for just a short time, I heard my friends talking about Jungian psychology and the theory of the Animus and Anima, which Jung developed. The Animus, they said, was a woman's internal man, who usually was supressed in our society because it was considered unfeminine to climb trees or to be too intellectual, or be interested in plumbing and business. The Anima, on the other hand, was a man's female part, who likewise had been ignored for cultural reasons, because big boys don't cry and men are expected to keep a macho image all the time.

The suppression of half of our natures leaves us crippled, dissatisfied, and dependent upon our partners to provide us with our other halves. The plot thickens: when we fall in love we project that internal male or female part, which is our soul, onto our lovers and actually fall in love with ourselves. This is a form of transference. But since we don't understand the process, and since we are split in too, the torture begins. Separation from the beloved is extremely painful, even for a few hours, as if some terrible loss has occurred, and when the relationship ends, as it inevitably does, one can go into an almost death-like state—terrific depression and suicidal tendencies. We have literally placed our soul in another's body, unconsciously, and when that person leaves, we are torn asunder.

Of course we recover, and the soul comes back into our own bodies, but since we are still not conscious of him or her, as soon as the proper object crosses the screen again, off we go into the same torturous mechanism. No wonder they call it *falling* in love.

I am also amazed at what we put up with when we are in love. No one in their right mind would let a friend or acquaintence slander them in public, physically hurt them, turn them away from their own needs and interests, or lead them across the country to a place where they have no friends and nothing to do. Yet ''lovers'' are constantly abusing each other in an infinite number of ways. You've watched them. You've done it yourself. When we are in love we believe we have the right to demand all sorts of things of our lovers that we would never demand from a friend, or let them demand of us. We have the notion that the lover should be at constant attention to our needs and desires and have our pleasure as their sole aim in life. We are livid if the lover gives emotional or physical attention to anyone else, or to their work, or even to their children. Most of the relationships I have witnessed become extremely destructive and confining after the initial rush. They become arenas for death, instead of life and growth, and luckily for us, they are short lived. It's as if some higher power intervenes and says, "I'm sorry, you can't have this relationship because it's harmful to your growth and evolution,"and *Bang!* it's over.

Several years after hearing my friends' stories I became very depressed at the end of a relationship, and went to see an Archetypal Psychologist. Through guided fantasy I first saw my Animus as a youth of about twenty-three, although I myself was thirty-nine. He said he was just starting out on his career, and although he was shy about presenting his ideas to the world, he thought he was on to some good ideas, and they were being well received. The Animus told me that he wanted me to give him more time for work, that he needed time to develop his ideas, and that I was so flakey about the business aspect of my life that I was interfering with him. I agreed to give him more time and more encouragement, because I could see that if he succeeded I would have more money to spend on things I wanted. We certainly didn't feel like lovers, or even friends, as I found him too young and inexperienced, and he found me too fat, and just not his type. (curiously enough I began losing weight several months later, for the first time in my life).

My second experience with my Animus was in his power to defend me, to protect me. I was in another relationship by that time in which I was again being treated badly. The "lover" was even in the habit of calling me names in public. My Animus came up one day screaming at the top of his lungs, "I hate that man! How dare you let him treat you that way! He has no respect for you—he treats you like a dog! You should be ashamed of yourself!" I agreed with him and moved away from the relationship.

He also chided me about being too nice, too

accommodating. After this conversation, I went home and wrote several letters to people who owed me money, saying that if I didn't hear from them within a certain period of time, I would take them all to court. I don't think I would have been able to do this if I had not allowed into my consciousness the force of this protective figure. My pattern would have been to be resentful, but let the debts drag on forever and eventually give up on them.

I also found him to be very critical of and competitive with men, and with other women too. In conversation I would find myself always trying to tell a better story than my companion, or if he or she told of a win or triumph in their lives I would come back immediately with a bigger win or triumph in *my* life.

When I became aware of this action of my Animus, I handled it by making a deal with him. I told him that I would make a supreme efort to give him whatever time he wanted for his work if he would lay off that critical, competitive, destructive stance in my relationships. It was difficult. Sometimes I imagined that he was a vicious bulldog crouched at my feet and ready to chew my friends or my lovers to bits. I imagined that I was holding him very tightly by his leash, almost choking him, forbidding him to attack, reminding him of our agreement.

I also experienced my Animus as a healthy little boy, who wanted to run in the woods and climb trees. I went out and bought myself a pair of tennis shoes so I could jump and climb better. One evening at a party I exchanged clothes with a man friend who was wearing a tank top and cutoffs and had a wonderful time dancing around in them, feeling (and looking) like a little boy.

One day, after complaining to my therapist that I just couldn't seem to earn a living, we had a session in which we fantasized a trip into the underworld to seek out my treasure, as if it were being withheld from me, just as in the ancient myths the hero or heroine goes in search of a treasure which is important to their lives but which is being guarded or hoarded by some fearsome beast.

So we imagined ourselves descending into Hades, the underworld, which Jung used to call the subconscious, crossing the river Styx, and setting out in search of my treasure.

The first thing I saw was the temple of Hades and Persephone. It looked like the cathedral of Notre Dame, and was very white and glowing. There was a long flight of stairs up to the entrance, and I knew they were inside. I was very much in awe and afraid to go in. After all, you don't just go waltzing up to the God of Death and his lady and say, "Hi! I've come for my treasure!" The therapist suggested that I fantasize an act of ritual purification, and I remembered that I had seen, outside of many temples in Japan, a stone receptacle with a bamboo dipper. I had been told that one purified oneself by taking a bit of the water and sloshing it around in one's mouth and spitting it on the ground. I tried it in the fantasy, but I was still afraid to go any further than the steps of the temple.

Suddenly, however, Hades and Persephone appeared at the entrance, came down the few steps that separated me from them, and each took a hand and walked me into the temple. At the instant they touched me I became a dwarf, a female dwarf, with long blond hair. "My god, I'm a dwarf!" I squawked.

Inside the temple they sat on their thrones and I stammered, "You know why I'm here?" "Yes," they nodded. "Look at me," I said, "I'm a dwarf, a cripple. My treasure has been denied me."

Persephone smiled and reached down into a pearl covered box that was by her feet. She offered me something from the box that looked like a communion wafer. She put it in my mouth and instantly, like Alice in Wonderland, I grew from a dwarf into a beautiful, shining, naked man, a wise hero.

Persephone acted like I was leaving. "You want me to leave?" I asked, dumbly. "Yes," she said. "I'm not supposed to ask you any questions?" "No, you have everything you need." I turned to go and the therapist broke in. "You know, Hades, being the God of Death, is usually reluctant for us to leave his kingdom." "Then I'd better ask his permission," I said, and turned to ask. "You may leave," he said, "because it is Persephone's wish."

So we ended the fantasy and the therapist said, "So what is your treasure?" "My Animus," I replied, and was surprised to notice that I could now imagine that the wise hero was sitting beside me on the couch with his hand on my thigh. He had beautiful hands and a beautiful muscular body, an Adonis. I felt wonderful having him there. "Now the next time you talk to him, ask him his name," the therapist advised. "GEORGE," said the man sitting next to me.

Once at home I sat down at my typewriter and asked him all the usual questions I have been asking the archetypal characters as I meet them. "What about my work? What about my relationships?" I imagined that he was standing by my desk. I asked the questions and typed the answers as he gave them. He said that the way to have the brilliance of falling in love and yet avoid the pitfalls, was to project him *consciously* into my lovers and take him back out whenever we are not physically together. He said that as long as I didn't leave him there, and maintained a good conscious connection to him, I would have the best relationships I have ever had with men.

I imagined him watching me as I put away the typewriter and changed my clothes. I could feel love coming from his heart to mine. He was so beautiful, and so adoring of me! I'd never had that experience with a man before. I also felt shy, virginal, in relation to him. He was always naked, and sometimes I was too shy to look at his genitals. "Would you like to come and talk to me while I make dinner?" I asked. "Sure," he said amiably, and we marched up the stairs.

I felt so comfortable having him there while I cooked—so relaxed, so cared for, so loved. My daughter came into the kitchen and we had a short conversation. She appeared to me to be the most beautiful young woman on earth, and the most charming. I told her so and she grinned with pleasure. My son came in too, and I felt relaxed and loving towards him.

That night a lover came over, one with whom I had a friendly, sexy, but not particularly romantic relationship. He also had a way of making love which I was finding increasingly uncomfortable and unsatisfactorfy and I had been trying to figure out how to steer him into some new tricks. As we began to make love, I imagined that George was inside his body. Since George was there, and I knew he wanted to serve me and give me whatever I wanted, I found myself explaining and showing my lover how to make love to me. I guided his hands, told him when to wait and when to move. I had permission at last to direct the experience and get what I wanted out of it. He was perfect. We both agreed afterward that it was the best lovemaking experience we'd ever had together.

The next day I set out on my usual hectic schedule. My pattern is to be anxious all day long about whether I will be on time for my appointments and whether I will be able to accomplish what I need to accomplish in a day's time. I run around in a state of generalized anxiety all day long. But on this particular day, as I turned on the ignition I imagined that George was sitting beside me in the car. He said, "This pattern of anxiety you have is seriously detrimental to your health, and moreover, when you're wound up like that there's no possibility for any creativity or insights to come through. The most important thing you can do right now is to get rid of that anxiety, and you'll do it by paying strict attention to the way your body feels. At the first twinge of anxiety you will stop what you're doing and find out what's making you worried or nervous, and if you can't talk yourself out of it, you'll have to stop and rest until your body calms down."

I knew he was right, and I paid attention. Every time I felt uptight during the day I stopped my whirling brain to find out what I was worried about. And I told myself things like, "Well, I can do that tomorrow," or "I'm not going to be uptight about being late," or whatever it took to make my muscles relax and my stomach stop churning. I also had a sense of well-being I had never felt with any regularity in my life, and certainly not felt at all for a long time.

Somewhere in the course of the day I realized that I was behaving as if I were *loved*. Like I always knew I would feel if I had someone to lean on, someone who cared about me and wanted to be with me, the lover, the soul mate, I had been seeking. I had my dream lover, my soul mate, right by my side, and I'd had him all along, but unconsciously. That sense of longing for fulfillment was gone, and in its place a sense of satisfaction and well-being, a security, a feeling of being loved. I realized that I could enjoy my kids because I was feeling loved and satisfied, instead of frustrated and pulled apart by their demands. I learned to allow *them* to love *me* and it seemed as if they had just been waiting there all along for me to allow them to do so.

Let's look at some of the ramifications of this experience. Standard sex therapy for women is to teach them to masturbate and find out what gives them orgasm. After that they can teach their lovers how to bring them to orgasm or simply do it themselves even though they are with a partner.

Most women have a lot of difficulty with this last part of the therapy. "How can I touch myself in front of a man?" "How can I tell him what to do to make me come?" "How can I make suggestions without making him angry and threatening his male ego?" She may feel a sense of the impossibility of getting a man to listen to her needs. She may believe that what she wants and needs is either not OK, or subordinate to the wants and needs of her man.

Most of us are aware that we continuously project our past conditioning and experiences onto the people and objects in our environment. We expect our lovers to treat us in a certain way, for example, based on our past experiences and conditioning. However, if a woman could contact her positive Animus and project him into her lover, as I did, then instantly the scene would change. The projection she is making on the universe would change, because her internal man, who adores her, would be willing and enthusiastic about doing whatever would give her more pleasure. She would develop the ability to ask for what she wants and ask for it in a way which gets a positive response from her physical partner.

There have been numerous payoffs for me in working with George. First of all, I've discovered that the masculine and feminine develop together. Like yin and yang, they are intertwined, interdependent. If the masculine nature has been inhibited, then the feminine won't develop either. For example, since George has been in my life I have begun dressing beautifully, have become softer and more receptive, more attractive, and much more successful with men. I no longer am waiting for a man to come and save me, financially or emotionally. I enjoy paying my own bills and looking after my own emotional needs. I used to lose lovers by being whiney and dependent, and this doesn't happen any more.

In addition, my relationship with my children improves daily. I am more able to appreciate them, to play with them, to just be with them, than I used to be. I am remembering that all my children really need from me is genuine heart-y love, and I am learning how to give it to them. It is a combination of the opening of my heart and the feelings of personal balance and satisfaction that comes from having met my soul mate, my Animus. This is not to say that I have lost interest in my lovers; quite the contrary. I'm saying that the soul mate is internal, not external. Prince Charming is George, not my lovers. They are just men, very dear men to me, who have their own souls to worry about and can't possibly take care of mine, or *be* mine, as suggested by the theory of soul mates. And this realization deepens and intensifies my relationships with them a thousand-fold.

George also gives me excellent advice in my relationships. Most recently I was putting all my love energy into a man who repeatedly told me that he didn't want a relationship with me. But I persisted, because my desire for him was very strong. One night after a party, when I expected to go home with him, I heard him asking another woman to be his partner for the night, and then heard that they had spent the entire weekend together. I was crushed, but I really had to admit that I had been warned. In the midst of my agony I decided to have a conversation with George and see if he could help.

He said, ''You're right. There's nothing that can replace a lover in the physical body. You need a man. You deserve a man; you're a beautiful woman. My being here doesn't prevent you from falling in love. You want him. It's OK to want him. He's a good man—but there's no accounting for tastes, because he doesn't seem to want *you*. He doesn't know what he's missing, but it's OK to want him, Margo. It's OK to want, period. See if you can find someone else to want.''

''But I want *him,*'' I wailed.

''But he doesn't want *you*. You are miserable, not because he has your soul, (I'm right here), but because he simply doesn't want you. It's a losing game. Find someone else. You think he's the only interesting guy in the world? There must be some others. You were happy with your last lover, remember? He wasn't brilliant and clever like this one, but he was a wonderful man and you loved him very much. It's OK to love, Margo, and if the one you love doesn't respond it's because of their fears. not because there's something lacking in your love. Keep trying. Stiff upper lip. Tomorrow's another day.''

Nowadays George soothes me on the few occasions when I'm lonely. He is also an excellent consultant on financial affairs, easing my fears, giving me ideas about how to handle my financial situation and new ideas about how to make money. I've started taking Kung Fu, and loving the strong masculine feelings it gives me. I imagine that it strengthens George too.

My therapist recently said that since my Animus was undeveloped, as well as unconscious, I had been in the past attracted to boyish men, men who could not take care of themselves and who related to me as if I were their mother. There is no possibility for a satisfying relationship between two adults if one is playing parent and the other is playing child. And since it is an archetypal relationship, the child (in this case a son) must grow up and leave the parent. My lovers were always leaving me.

The theory was that if I could get George to grow up then I could attract a *man* into my life instead of an adult boy. Of course growing up means learning how to earn a living, something I have always had difficulty with. It also means being in charge of one's own life, being the final authority on what needs to be done and what to do. George also made the remark once, in a fantasy, that I should stop seeing him all the time as naked, because only babies are naked, and that I should think about what I wanted him to wear. So I bought a number of men's magazines and cut out pictures of clothes I like, and imagined George wearing them.

My workshop participants occasionally ask about soul mates and so I have begun giving them a guided fantasy in which they meet their Animus or Anima, and this introduce them to their soul mates rather than talking about them. The fantasy is simple, and you may try it if you like. Imagine that you are in a beautiful place, one that you have actually been to, or one you make up. Begin your fantasy by just walking around in that place, noticing what animals and plants and smells and sounds are there. Pick a place in which you are alone and there are no other people.

Then imagine that you can see, at a distance, someone coming towards you, someone of the opposite sex. (Don't worry if you can't see anything. Some people aren't visual in this sort of exercise, but they can hear and feel). As the person approaches, you can feel that he/she loves you with a selfless love which we have rarely experienced on this plane. When he/she gets close enough you may hug if you wish, and begin to talk or play with this person. Ask the person's name. Ask any questions that come to your mind. Take the opportunity to engage in some non-verbal play. Let the meeting take whatever form it does, and end it when you feel it is ended. Thus you will begin your relationship to your Animus or Anima. Have frequent meetings and conversations with him/her. Ask for advice in your relationships and your work. When you are ready begin loving and making love. Masturbate while you have this fantasy.

Some people, when doing this exercise, will see a current or former lover. This is because the Animus or Anima has been projected into that lover and is still there, even though the affair may be over. If this happens, you will have to ask that person to move over so you can meet your true Animus or Anima. First ask them why they came to see you and if they have anything to tell you, and when your conversation is complete, ask them to just step aside so you can see the being standing behind them.

Others meet a being who doesn't seem like a lover at all, or doesn't measure up to their standards of a soul mate or an ideal lover. One participant in a workshop met a 147 year old Russian woman with a broom. Another met a dark, ominous cloud which hung about in a tree and frightened her. In her conversation with this being, she realized that she had been dominated all her life by her masculine nature, and had never been able to develop her feminine side. She had been successful in business, but had never had a relationship with a man, saying, "I never know how to act when I am expected to be a woman." She was dressed in clothes that were old and raggedy, and her hair was scraggly and unkempt. The next day she came to the workshop in a long skirt and a peasant blouse with her hair piled on top of her head. Everyone in the group was amazed at the change. She looked radiant...and feminine.

In Haiti, I understand, there is a mystical cult which uses the relationship with the internal man or woman as a source of power. The student keeps a beautifully decorated room in the house for the internal woman or man. Once a week the student spends the night in this room, alone with the soul mate, making love.

For those who are interested in developing themselves as Androgynous beings, that is, persons who have full access to both their masculine and feminine attributes, I am convinced that the first step is to make acquaintance with the internal man or woman, and it is through this relationship that the balance of masculine and feminine in the psyche will develop.

Popular songs chronicle our predicament with love and relationships:

"I can't live if living is without you..."

"I need you like flowers need the rain..."

"I know I'll never love this way again..."

"I only have eyes for you..." (Not my work or my family or my friends).

"Where are you now when I need you?...If you don't come back there'll be nobody left in this world to hold me tight..."

"All I need is you..."

Our relationships as a rule are not only unsatisfactory but destructive. We look to the relationship to solve our problems and make us feel whole, and this is impossible, except for the short period of the initial rush. Having become couples, we sacrifice our deepest needs for expression and creative work because of the belief that if we only stick with the relationship all our needs will be met. ("All you need is love"). We become addicted to that other person, miserable, hanging in there even though it is obvious to everyone but ourselves that we are wasting our time.

The idea that "All we need is Love" is one of the most foolish and destructive ideas in our culture. We need love, of course. Babies die without it and adults don't fare much better. But we also need creativity, a sense of belonging, the ability to make judgments (the true function of the intellect) and health, and no doubt other things as well. If all we have is love, we are going to be in really bad shape. If you all you have is love, you can get killed. I speak from experience, having walked through life with an open heart for several years and having it stepped on repeatedly because I lacked courage and discrimination.

Relationships have a chance of being successful if each person in the relationship is self-centered, that is, focused on her/his own needs, and on becoming acquainted with the internal masculine or feminine self. One must also have one's own creative work and a sex life with oneself in addition to the sex in the relationship.

When I no longer come from need I can come from love. I can be a good companion, a loving companion, a good lover. As long as I am expecting my partner to do the work for me that I can only do for myself—finding my own soul, my own joy, my own creative work, my own means of expression—the relationship hasn't a chance. But when I establish a relationship with my true soul mate, my Animus, there is a possibility of success.

Chapter Six

More on Relationships

The purpose of romantic relationships is ecstasy. Not security, not status, not being taken care of, not paying the bills, not emotional support. The purpose of romantic relationships is ecstasy. Ecstasy can be created by using sexual energy as I have described.

I think we can safely say that most couples experience ecstasy infrequently, if at all, and usually at the beginning of the relationship. For the rest of the relationship, the couple stares at each other across their chicken pies, angry, disillusioned, bored, and wondering what went wrong. Many separate; many stay right there with the chicken pie for the rest of their lives.

First of all, we do not experience ecstasy because it is a function of sexuality and most of us, as explained before, are almost completely shut off sexually.

Secondly, we become enmeshed in the demands of a psyche which does not know how to love and which is specifically ruled by an unconscious, demanding, and critical inner man or woman. We demand that the external lover be perfect, be prince or princess charming, instead of knowing that the only perfect lover is inside. The only one who can always love you perfectly, take care of you perfectly, is yourself.

It simply happens that two people are able to generate more energy together to use for this alchemy than each one alone. But the catch is, that unless each partner can generate energy *alone*, and can *relate* to the other person, the energy is unavailable. The first thing we shut off when we are angry or disappointed in a relationship is the sex.

What does it mean *to relate?* I think we are able to relate when our hearts are open to each other. In a romantic relationship our bodies are open to each other also. Aside from the initial transference of falling in love, most people have no access to the energy and joy of the heart because they have no alchemy. When the transference is over they cannot love.

You will find, if you use your sexual energy to bombard your heart chakra, that it will be easier and easier for you to love—your children, your friends, and those you select as your lovers.

You will also find that you are more and more content within yourself and less in need of love. It's the *need* of love that keeps it away. Love comes from inside, not from outside. I've come to the point where I enjoy my own company as much as any one else's, so I'm not needy any more. And since I don't come from need, I don't scare people away.

The next thing you will notice as you work with this method is that most people have no access to their hearts whatsoever. What they call love is transference, sex, and emotional and physical demands.

Every man needs to develop his internal woman, that is, his sense of beauty, his emotional responses, his creative muse. He canot demand that the external woman, his lover, be for him what he can only be for himself.

Every woman needs to develop her internal man, her sense of who she is and what she can do in the world in addition to bearing children. She needs to feel herself as a force, a yang force, an effective force in the world, and not ask her man, her external man, to be these things for her.

The plot thickens because there are men whose internal woman is more developed than his maleness, and women whose internal man dominates and prevents her feminine attributes from developing. I was a woman who had adopted the cultural stance that male is best, thereby stifling my female attributes, but not really allowing the male ones to develop either, because after all, I am a woman, and to do so would be unfeminine. Total paralysis.

Another reason relationships fail is that we try to make them the center of our lives. I would like to suggest that a passionate relationship is a corner, one fourth of the relatedness of a human being.

There are four archetypes of relationship:
1) Brother/sister/friend
2) Passionate beloved
3) Parent/child

4) Self/creative work, vocation/health

What happens to us when we fall in love is that we neglect everything else and get rid of everything which interferes with the relationship, because ''love (romantic love) is all we need.''

We need all four forms of relatedness. Just as we feel lost without a lover, we feel lost or incomplete when we have no creative work, poor relationships with our parents or children, or no friends.

I have two children, and I am discovering that they are built-in lovers. Unless you treat them really badly they love you no matter what you do, and even then, they love you along with the hate and anger. They are non-stop-forever-to-the-grave-and-beyond lovers. Ordinarily we don't have sex with them, but we can have with them everything else we have with our lovers: fun times, touching and hugging, caring, intensity. We yell at each other when we are angry and it feels good. I can't tell you why I never discovered these two lovers of mine before, but my guess is that as *my* heart opened more and more through doing the sexual energy exercise, I just happened to begin to feel *their* hearts, which had been open all the time. Thank goodness it's not too late to develop a relationship with them before they grow up and move away.

We have talked about the relationship with self in terms of making love to oneself and self love. As I have grown with this method and watched it work in my system over the last five years, I see that my relationship with myself, and especially my creative work, depends on the joy I have in being alone.

I find people to be almost incredulous when I tell them how I need and enjoy my alone time. Most people have no idea what it feels like to be alone. They work, come home and take care of their families or socialize with their friends. Weekends are taken up with more chores and friends. Sleep is the only alone time they have, and then they do not investigate their dreams.

They are afraid of being alone. We are taught to believe that there is something wrong with a child or adult who seems to prefer to be alone. It's true that we need the other forms of relatedness, friends and lovers, and that most people have difficulty relating to other people. It is not true that people should not want to be alone. Just as having no friends is a sign of sickness, or a lack in a person's life, the inability to be alone and find inspiration and healing therein, is a sickness and a lack.

What do I do in my favorite alone days? Well, I get up when I like, do my exercises and my tai chi, take a long bath, give myself a full body massage, take myself out to eat something wonderful or fix something special for myself at home. Perhaps I write an article, or a few pages in my journal, or spend part or all of the day in the country letting the rocks and trees heal me and teach me.

When I am in a romantic relationship my alone time gains even more importance. It's too easy to get lost in a relationship. One can lose one's identity, one's direction in life, one's creative work, one's sense of self. One can be seemingly at the constant beck and call of the relationship. *We* replaces *I* in thought and deed. All the more reason to separate, to feel oneself again as a separate entity, a being complete in oneself. *The Prophet* says, "Let there be spaces in your togetherness." Let passionate relationships exist alongside careers, friends, children.

I also had a wonderful experience this last winter with celibacy. Being fed up with my relationships as they were at the moment, I decided to take a vow of celibacy and spend the winter entirely alone, not making love to anyone but myself. In previous years I could not have done so, any more than I could have fasted. *What? Live without a man? Without partner sex? Why, I would die, or go crazy, wouldn't I?*

To my surprise it was one of the most satisfying experiences or experiments, of my life. The most significant result of the vow was that, since I was not looking for a man, my attention was on myself. I did more writing and more creative work during this time than in any other period of my life. Since my attention was not outside my body, outside my own system, it could be used here, inside, for me. Mystical disciplines often require that their devotees be celibate. In addition to the loss of energy through orgasm, as I mentioned earlier, there is a loss of energy through having one's *attention* focused elsewhere than on oneself.

Another discovery in the last few years is what I call *friends who fuck.* I'm not much into one night stands, although they're fun occasionally, and I'm not a swinger.

But I've found that I have several friends whom I deeply love, with whom I will never, for one reason or other, be *in love,* but with whom I can have great sex and great caring and fondness.

Friends who fuck are different from lovers. Since they aren't in love they are free to see other people, to make love with other people, and to pursue their own lives. They miss each other deeply if they are separated, but do not clutch at each other the way lovers do. They make fewer demands, put fewer "trips" on each other than lovers. Friends who fuck are a lot lighter than lovers and they have more fun.

Friends who fuck are often people I wouldn't or shouldn't fall in love with. For example, one of my friends is a man with whom I have great fun and great sex, but who could never be a forever lover because I would not allow myself to fall in love with a person who is eleven years younger and three inches shorter than I. He also plays the archetypal role of son and expects his older women lovers to play mother, and through long and painful experience I have discovered that this doesn't work.

Another friend is married. His life with his wife is dull, but he has a kid, and divorce is expensive. We get together about once a month, when I'm not involved in a heavy romantic relationship, and we have a wonderful time. The sex is excellent and we are very fond of each other. But I would be nuts to fall in love with a married man. (Also learned from bitter experience).

And then there's Rick, my satyr, one of the sexiest, most playful men I have ever met. He has fits of depression and violent affairs with women, none of which I am interested in getting involved with, but when he's feeling good, and we get together, it's hot.

With a group of friends like this, with my joyful alone time, with my creative work and the blossoming love for my children, I am never at a loss for love, even though I may not have a beloved.

With friends I can care for and make love to, there is always someone I like calling me, or if I need someone, there is always someone to call. One of the problems with monogamy is that all your eggs are in one basket. If something upsets the basket your supply of love is gone If your partner is depressed or out of town, or needs to be alone, or is mad at you, *whammo!* No love and no sex. If monogamy is agreed on by a couple then having a personal sex life, being able to enjoy making love to oneself, is especially important.

When I have a beloved I usually don't want anyone else, but when I'm coming down from one of my tragic affairs I can call any one of a number of friends and say, "Hey, Baby, come and take care of me!" and a beautiful man will appear at my door, give me a massage, take me out to dinner, make love to me beautifully and caringly, and cuddle with me all night long, even if I haven't seen him for a while or if the sex has dropped out of our relationship because I have been *in love* with someone else.

Friends who fuck is an expansion of one of the archetypes of relationship, brother/sister/friend. It's love without being in love. It has not been used in our culture much because of fear of pregnancy. It would not have been convenient for society to have lots of children with no fathers. Lineage and property were better managed if each lady had her children by one man. But reliable birth control, for all its drawbacks, has changed our sex lives and our social lives radically. I never have to have a child I don't want, so I am free to accept more than one brand of DNA, since it won't be connecting with mine.

There is always a falling out of love, an end to the transference. If we are lucky we will fall out of love into friendship and ecstasy, because we will have understood the process and developed our sexual relationship so that it has created a pleasure bond between us and opened our hearts to each other. It's as if the transference gives us a boost to get things started, and if the heart and the sexuality can be opened, the relationship can move into a new phase.

What relationships are about is ecstasy. If your relationship with your beloved isn't fun, take a look at it. If it isn't ecstatic, take a look at it. Why are you together? For security? For sex? For financial reasons? You may decide to stay in your relationship for these reasons, but at least be honest with yourself.

There are a few popular songs which describe healthy relationships, and this is one I like:

"You're not a king, you're not an angel, you're a man. I'm not a queen, I'm a woman. Take my hand."

Chapter Seven

About My Teacher

I decided to write a chapter about the man who gave me the technique I teach, because I found people to be fascinated whenever I would tell stories about him.

I met him first as a Rebirthing client, and when he called for that first appointment he sounded so strange and distant and depressed that I asked a man friend of mine to sit in on the session with me. For the first and only time in my career as a Rebirther, I felt I needed some big strong man there, just in case.

When he arrived on his huge black chopper and stood in my living room with his motorcycle helmet and leather jacket, I thought his outfit didn't fit his personality—fragile, scared, soft. "This guy can't be a Hell's Angel," I thought.

We went upstairs to the small bathroom where I was accustomed to holding people in a huge old bathtub and encouraging them to breathe. He announced that he could not be rebirthed that way because he was too sensitive and needed to have some distance between his physical body and everyone else's. So he asked us to sit on the other side of the room and draw all our energy into ourselves so that none would touch him. He also anounced that he could not breathe the way I was asking him to, and he breathed his own way. After twenty minutes or so he got out of the tub and reported that he was finished, that it was a wonderful experience, and paid me fifty dollars.

As he was leaving, he noticed that I had my legs crossed and told me to uncross them, saying that he was a Tantra Master and knew a lot about energy. My eyes popped, as I had been searching for reliable information on Tantra for several years, unsuccessfully. I asked him to teach me. He looked up in the air to his left, as if listening to something, and then said, "OK. Come to my place tomorrow afternoon and we'll begin."

He lived in a tiny, bare house in the country just outside of San Diego. The first time we met we sat on the floor in the kitchen and looked into each other's eyes. He touched my forehead and a wave of laughter came from somewhere and shook my body all over. Then a wave of sadness, and I was ready to cry. My body felt intensely energized and focused on itself, cognizant of itself. "I think you've had enough for today." he said. "I'd like you to lie down in the hammock outside and rest."

To get to the hammock we had to pass to the right side of the tree instead of the left, he said, "because the energy is better on this side." I lay in the hammock, not dozing, but somewhere between waking and sleeping, listening to him moving around the house and shed, and began having sexual fantasies about him. After awhile he came out to the hammock and said, "Your thoughts are disturbing me at my work. Will you please go home now."

He added, "I'm going to give you an exercise which I want you to do every day for three months, which is, to masturbate until the point where you know that one more stroke will make you come, take your hand away, and allow the energy to come up to your heart. You can repeat the cycle as often as you like."

I stumbled toward my car, stoned from the experiences of the afternoon and stunned at being asked to leave so abruptly, and as I was about to drive off, thought to ask, "When should I come again?" "You'll know when to come," he said. "But..." I stammered. "You'll know. Now leave."

And I did know. A couple of weeks later on a lovely spring day I was thinking about him in a warm and loving way and knew somehow that it was time to go for another visit. I had also been doing the exercise as he instructed and noticing a warm trickle of energy coming up to my chest each time, charging my chest and heart and making me feel wonderful.

He welcomed me as if he had been expecting me and said that he would like to do some balancing of my energy so that we could be together more comfortably, that is, so that I would not offend his physical sensitivity. He asked me to wait in the kitchen while he did something to the energy in his bedroom, altering it

somehow so we could work in there. After a few minutes
he invited me in. The bedroom was as spartan as the
kitchen—nothing on the walls, nothing in the room
except a bed, a Franklin stove, and a brass basket for
magazines or wood, which was empty. He asked me to
take off my clothes and lie down on the bed. He touched
me gently in various places, apparently following some
plan of balancing my energy, and each time he touched
me for a few seconds, he wiped his fingers with a clean
pink Kleenexes and dropped it on the floor. Some time
later there was a huge mound of pink Kleenexes on the
floor. He explained that he had to keep wiping the negative energy off his fingers so that it wouldn't unbalance
his own energy.

When he was through he asked if I'd like to make
love. I said yes. I was still lying on the bed. He took off
his clothes, and looked at my breasts with the most
intense love and adoration I have ever experienced.
Then, without touching me, he leaned over and just let a
little warm air from his mouth touch one nipple. An
intense rush of sexual energy filled my chest. Then he
came closer and just barely touched the tip of his cock to
my vulva and the same kind of intense, sexual rush filled
the lower half of my body. He instructed me to lie
perfectly still, without touching him or myself, keeping
all my energy and attention in my head instead of my
genitals or other erotic areas, and fucked me for just a
couple of minutes, barely touching me anywhere else
than my genitals.

Having imagined long, langorous, affectionate Tantra sessions, I was shocked when he came in a couple of
minutes, rolled over, and told me it was time to leave.
"Some Tantra session," I thought, feeling cheated.
"More like a slam-bam-thank-you-ma'am than a reli-
gious experience." But when I tried to stand up I noticed the energy in my body. I felt like I had been
plugged into an electric socket. I was vibrating all over,
the energy starting from my genitals and going in waves
to every corner of my body. I had difficulty standing
up and my vision was altered, as if I had taken acid.
I was impressed. Not bad for a two-minute fuck. In slow
motion I put on my clothes and headed for my car. I
didn't ask when I should come back. The feelings lasted
for the rest of the day and the evening, and I continued

with the exercise he'd given me, practicing every day.

In succeeding months I began to learn more about him. He was psychic and could always tell what was going on with me. Every so often I would put out the thought that I'd like to see him, and within a day or two I'd meet him on the street or find him at my door. If I was depressed he'd come and say, "I heard you needed me." He told me that he had taught himself to be clairvoyant, clairaudient, and clairsentient, and that his knowledge of Tantra had come partly from experiencing his own super-sensitive body and partly from extra-terrestrial beings who were his teachers. He often talked to them when I was present, especially to ask if I were ready for a new technique or not. I heard nothing and saw no one.

His sensitivity had some drawbacks, however. For one thing he couldn't walk in certain areas of a room, or any space, when the energy configurations were too uncomfortable for him. He also had great difficulty being around other people because their energy interfered with his own, or unbalanced it in some way. He explained that sometimes he had to spend months alone, allowing his teachers to rebalance his energy for him. He usually looked worried and uncomfortable.

Once he explained that the ideal relationship between two people was one in which all the chakras, or energy centers of the body, were connected. When we made love he would evaluate the experience in terms of how many chakras had been connected, for example "We were connected all the way to the throat chakra that time." After awhile I began noticing that I connected with people using various centers; for example, I have some friends with whom I have an intense loving relationship and some intellectual contact, but no sex. Occasionally I have had sexual contact and connected nowhere else. All the relationships are good, but I would agree with him that the more areas of the total human being which can connect at one time, the higher and more satisfying the relationship.

Once, on a rare occasion when he was relaxed and affectionate with me, we lay in the sunshine in a green grassy park, and he counselled me about money. I was a struggling beginner with just a few clients and a lot of financial worries. He encouraged me to know that "the teachers'' would take care of me and my children. About six months after my relationship with him ended, I met the man to whom this book is dedicated. He loved me and my work enough to encourage me, work for me, and lend me money to get my work across to the public.

Then my teacher told me the story of how he came to be on ''disability'' as he called it. His wife had been pushing him to get a job and earn some money, and he realized that the only thing he could do to earn money was to give an erotic type of massage, and the only people who were interested were people like his friends and fellow healers, who couldn't pay for it.

So he went to some government agency and asked to be put on welfare because there was nothing he could do to earn a living. He was given a couple of sessions with a psychiatrist to determine if he could work. In the first one the psychiatrist announced that he was perfectly OK to work, so he got worried and asked his teachers to help him. ''I didn't know what I was going to say, or how I was going to do it, but I knew I had to get on welfare. There was no other way to support my family.'' So he went for the second interview and during the interview, ''Babaji came and took me out of my body and took me up to the ceiling, where I looked around and down at my body while the psychiatrist was trying to talk to me. Since I couldn't talk to him very well at that distance, he decided I was definitely crazy and put me not only on welfare but on state disability. So you see, you will be taken care of too.''

He also counselled me to stop worrying about my relationships with men. ''Soon, very soon, your energy will be so attractive that you'll have plenty of lovers.''

He constantly repulsed my efforts to establish a relationship with him, and got very angry when he thought I was ''attaching my mating cords'' to him. I never knew exactly what he meant, but it sounded like what Don Juan talks about, as if there are energy waves which can be projected out of our bodies to other people, in this case from the lower belly. He always asked me to leave when he felt that this was happening.

Towards the end of our association, which lasted about a year, I met a man I was interested in, and told my teacher, on one of our visits, that I was going to visit this new man in Hawaii. He said that he wanted me to have the best possible relationship with this new man and for that reason he would cut all the psychic and physical ties we had to each other so that I would be free. I couldn't see or feel what he did, but I found myself *very* reluctant to leave his house that day, and as I drove towards the freeway I was overwhelmed by waves of energy and grief, so much so that I couldn't drive, and pulled the car over to the side of the country road, where I sobbed and shook uncontrollably for twenty minutes. I had to stop once more on the freeway on the way home, for the same reason.

The last time I saw him we couldn't seem to relate at all. I had a terrible headache and couldn't stay next to him in bed. We yelled unkind things at each other and he jumped out of bed, put on his clothes, and left. I never saw him again.

Chapter Eight

Reports From Students

Whenever one proposes a new theory, no matter how beautiful it seems to the mind, one must find out, by patient experimentation, if it really works. The changes that have taken place in me might be the result of something other than the technique I teach, or, it may be that even though the alchemy is taking place in me, I will never be able to teach anyone else. So it's important to me to maintain contact with my students to see how they are doing.

In each workshop there are only a handful of people who take the exercise as a meditation and do it regularly and get results. I have heard from quite a few of them and the results are all positive. Most of them are where I was about two years ago and will presumably experience everything I have experienced if they continue.

The others, who do not use the exercise, I assume have such heavy prohibitions against pleasure and masturbation that they just can't bring themselves to do the exercise. Some have said as much. I suggest that they consider sex therapy.

Besides the positive results which I would expect from my students, changes patterning my own, they have had other positive experiences which I did not expect. I will quote some of their letters.

"I used to have severe menstrual cramps and lower back pain even when I wasn't on my period. Now I find that if any pain comes on, all I have to do is bring the energy from my pelvic area up to my heart, by using your exercise, and the pain goes away. I am delighted. Thank you! I think that pain was just blocked sexual energy."

"I didn't mention it at the workshop because I was too embarrassed, but I used to have a problem with premature ejaculation. I would come almost as soon as I got hard. I have found that the homework exercise has given me gradually the ability to tolerate more and more sexual energy in my body so that now I can stay hard as long as I like—almost indefinitely. I feel like a man for the first time in my life.''

"I feel so much better since the workshop, so much more alive. I have a lot more vitality and I'm much more willing to say what I want at work and at home, and I get what I want more often! My friends say I'm getting more and more beautiful, but I am too shy to tell them it's because of my masturbation. Anyway, I'm happy with my secret.''

"My sexual experiences have become very psychic. When I become connected to a person sexually these days, we reach a unity space I never thought possible. We visit past lives together, we read each others' thoughts, we become one in a magical and marvelous way. I also have a warm heat in my belly almost all the time. I feel wonderful.''

I have greater understanding of myself and others. I am more out front, stronger, truer to myself and others, more assertive, and more inwardly motivated—following *my* path more clearly.''

"I want to tell you that ever since your workshop my life has accelerated in pace tremendously. My husband is changing too, growing a lot with my catalytic effect. My relationships work well and there's much joy and love in my life. You were certainly a great catalyst for me to expand and not hold back on my energy, which is more whole and flowing now. Thank you always.''

"I now have a much higher awareness of my sexual energy. I've gotten rid of a lot of sexual hangups and have started to center my life. My *impotency* has disappeared, and my partner and I have started being one.''

"I am in the process of redefining orgasm. I find that it has many levels. I have had multiple orgasms and orgasms without ejaculation. For the first time in my life I am totally satisfied with my sexuality—I am no longer led around by my cock. I also feel my heart beginning to stir and open, which makes me very happy.''

"I am experiencing a rising of energy to the heart. It is a very positive feeling—a sense of openness and flowing, a sense of *nowness*. I feel very positive and much more open. I experience what you said in your quote—everything and everyone is loveable and beautiful to me. I also experience less fear of encounters with the opposite sex, and I am now asking for and trying to initiate relationships with women. Before the workshop I was not doing this at all, and I was always alone. I experience my heart opening and my personal magnetism developing, both very intensely.''

''My life went uphill after I attended your workshop, and has continued to climb. My sex life has been much fuller and deeper. (Perhaps I should say total?) Many of the things I learned in the workshop have helped me and added to my personal growth. My relationships have improved greatly and are of greater sensuality. Sex is more gratifying for me and my partner. My ability to have more orgasms per session has increased, and I am not worried about performance. It is unexplainable, but somehow I feel a new understanding of myself and people around me. It just grew from within. I feel love generating inside me and people like me more too. It is easy for me to meet people now. I'm really much more into life now than I ever have been.''

''When I bring the energy up to my heart the transfer of energy is apparent and pleasurable. When I do have an orgasm it is *very* fulfilling. I have a special new lover, a very deep sharing and growing with her.''

''Since your workshop I've been getting affirmations from my partners for slowing down the sexual act and being with the sensations without focusing on orgasm. My heart is continually opening and relationships with more and more people are flowing. Also sexual partners are available and more are willing to play 'Tantra' sex.''

''I've always loved my husband very much, but now I love him with my hands and my body. Your workshop opened me to my true sexual potential and I am delighted. So is he!''

One person, Jim Punkre, said the workshop had prompted him to write erotic poetry, and sent a sample:

The Nymph and the Satyr

Sweet, sensual wood nymph—
you wore a garland of daisies

in your hair
and I declare
you floated among water lilies
as frogs leaped
and dragonflies crept
over your milk-white
moonlit skin.

From the forest a satyr dared
approach
from the cover where he had watched
until he could control
his desire no longer.
Coarse and brutish,
his muscles tense
in goatish rut
he curled back his lips
and sucked the evening's heat
through the gaps in his sharp teeth.
Cock-hard, I saw, the snake
within him push outward
toward you
toward your lily thighs,
toward the folded lips of your secret crimson poppy
toward the honey-lined chambers of
glistening pink, deep within
your soft sea shell.

Already his aroma was on you,
circling you,
caressing you,
tickling you,
beconing and teasing you,
waiting over and through you
like a magnetic breeze that
pulled you;
like opium smoke
that drugged you;
like the oil of coconut
so sweet and sticky
as it clung to you—
gumming up the tidy, neat, orderliness
of your haven,
coating everything in
wanton abandon
and carnal surrender.

and Self Love

I saw it all.
I saw him set fire to your floral arrangements.
your pristine gardens,
your earthly Eden.
I saw you join him
in that place
by the pond
where small fish nibbled your toes,
and flies scratched your nose.
I saw the water's edge muddy
as your ripples made waves,
as your sobs floated up into the night,
as his thick, throaty laughter
turned to pleasure grunts,
as his hard, warty, leather sword
poked and punched,
pulled and pierced and pummeled
and swelled and throbbed and burned
inside you
and
then
burst!
with blood-hot
torrents
that uncoiled from some dark place
deep in the pit of his groin.
And
I saw the slick
of your mixed juices
bubble on the water's surface
carried out
by the ripples
still
moving over the pond
though you
were now
still
and he was now gone—
vanished back into
the smell of leaf mold and bark
and decaying life.
Gone, gone...
save for the limp, soaked
garland you wore in your hair
and the
daisies
crushed into the mud
at the water's edge.

Masturbation, Tantra

Masturbation, Tantra

Chapter Nine

The Theory Behind It All

One must first understand that "cosmic" states require changes in the body and psyche and are the result of an internal alchemy. The way this alchemy works is that we add energy to our system in such amounts and with such persistance that the internal changes take place and the chakras, or energy centers of the body, open, producing the experiences we call higher states of consciousness.

There are many ways of adding energy to the system. The method I teach is one. Systems of martial arts and meditation, bioenergetics, jogging, and many of the other New Age disciplines add energy to the system also and may result in similar changes.

There are many people these days pursuing the New Age disciplines, and thus there are more and more people experiencing expanded states of consciousness. It is helpful, when exploring new territory, to have a map. The following is loosely drawn from "The Levels of Consciousness" which I heard in a lecture at Arica, a mystical school to which I belong. The original was the work of Arica's founder, Oscar Ichazo.

THE LEVELS OF CONSCIOUSNESS
(Awake, or Objective Levels)
Unity
Pure Love
Pure Action
Wisdom
The Objective Witness

(Asleep, or Subjective Levels)
Psychic Panic, Suicide
Despair
Philosopher/Charlatan

Saint Ego/False Freedom
Society
Beliefs and Conditioning

We shall begin by discussing the lowest two levels, those of beliefs and society. Until recently all but a few human beings lived their entire lives on these two levels of consciousness. Our beliefs and conditioning are almost all inadequate to describe the world around and within us. Our emotional states are here also—our lonliness, fear, and anger. On the level of society we obey traffic signals, pay the mortgage, go to college, get married, clean up the kitchen.

Throughout one's history of following meditation, or the spiritual path, one will have brief experiences above the line, which act like cosmic carrots to keep the horse plodding along the path. The Big Bang theory of enlightment is incorrect. All one notices is that one is spending more and more time above the line, and less and less time below.

The first state above the line is called The Objective Witness. This is the experience of "being in the world but not of the world," of knowing that one is not one's body, not one's emotions, not one's personality. Since it is an experience and a level of consciousness, it cannot be learned by "watching one's thoughts" or any other technique. It just comes, all by itself, as a result of the internal changes that are taking place because one has been adding energy to the system.

Wisdom is the next level. I was a philosophy major in college, and studied Epistemology, or theories of Knowledge: "how we know what we know." It was never suggested that knowing was an experience I would have when an energy center in my forehead began to work, a level of consciousness.

The next level is Pure Action. This is "non-doing"— action without thought. Samurai warriors, artists, dancers, and many people who are not in the mystical tradition, have these experiences. I have it in sex—when the energy takes over and I am just being moved without thinking where my hands should go or what to do next. No marriage manual can get you to this point—it is not something that is taught; it is something that happens. It is a level of consciousness. I can also have the experience when I am dancing—my body will enter a space of movement which is usually very beautiful and expressive, but I never plan the movements. My mind is not running the show, only watching it. It's a beautiful, ecstatic experience, one to be remembered and sought after.

Pure Love feels like romantic love only there is no particular object. One is in love with the trees, the sidewalk, whatever happens to present itself, or whomever. One not only loves, one *is* love. It is *agape* or universal love, as opposed to *eros,* romantic or personal love.

The level called unity is the experience, which includes the body that the universe is of one substance. It is the enlightenment experience most talked about by mystical theoreticians, and of course cannot be talked about at all, because it is a non-verbal experience. I have this experience each time I raise my sexual energy up in my body, and also in orgasm.

Most of the experiences I have had "above the line" have been a direct result of the system I use and teach, of raising the sexual energy.

For those of you who have made it through the theory section this far, I would like to add that mysticism is extremely practical. It is not at all a matter of meditating and chanting forever in a cave by yourself with no reference to the world of finance or relationships. For example, if I know that I can add and subtract energy to and from my system, then when I am lonely, or angry, or afraid, I can add some energy to my system and get to the jet set level, where I will probably put on my best duds and go dancing, or take on a new lover. I will be in a different conscious space, with new thoughts and new behaviors. And the value of becoming more loving, more brilliant, more creative, and more intuitive, should be obvious.

It should be added that the body is the antenna for all this energy which is being pumped into the system and most of us begin with bodies which are, metaphorically, made of chewing gum instead of the copper wire that is needed to conduct the high voltage we are talking about. I encourage my students to work consciously towards eliminating the tension in the body, making it as healthy and strong and resilient as possible. Diet, massage, relaxation techniques, and martial arts such as T'ai Chi are important. Adding energy to the system will only make you more uncomfortable if your vehicle is loaded with tension and disease.

I am learning the meaning of "the body is your temple." My body is the place in which I worship, and with which I experience expanded states of consciousness.

However, if one participates in any of the above mentioned disciplines, or raises the sexual energy repeatedly in the body, there will be a time of break-through in which the person will see herself/himself as being separate from or above the rules of society and released to some extent from conditioning and negative emotional states. He/she has added enough energy to the system that some changes have taken place and she/he operates part of the time, at least, in this new level of consciousness. Her/his behavior will probably change also. There may be a divorce, or a dropping out of college or quitting of a job. One may jump in a van and take off across the country to find—lord knows what. The jet set is here, and rock stars, and there may be a lot of money. It is called Saint Ego, or False Freedom because it is only the first level above Society, and the person usually thinks he/she is special or enlightened, and in actuality it is only the beginning.

The Philosopher/Charlatan is the seminar leader, the teacher, the false guru. They think they understand how the universe works and proceed to push their theories onto everyone else. Here are the true believers of all the New Age disciplines. Here we sit for hours and discuss our theories, absorbed in them completely. We know we are on a higher level of consciousness because we can feel it—there is so much energy in these discussions! The catch is that at this level we can't know the answers to our questions because our information about the universe and human personality is being filtered through our beliefs and conditioning. We are still below the line—in subjective or asleep levels of consciousness. Wisdom, or Knowledge, is above the line. It is a level of consciousness, not something that can be taught in the way arithmetic can be taught.

If one continues one's meditation, or whatever discipline has been producing these changes, the next energy level is that of despair. One believes that all one's work has been in vain, that the goal, whatever it may be, is unobtainable, that nothing can be known. The person in this state knows that he/she knows nothing, unlike the person in the level below, and can make her/him/self very unpopular by telling others (truthfully) that they don't know what they are talking about. It is very painful and unpleasant to be inside one's psyche at these times. One is desperate and isolated from other people, and the possibility of communication is almost non-existant. Friends try to cure you, make you feel better, take you to therapy, but something tells you that nothing is going to resolve the internal discomfort, certainly not therapy or any of the things that have worked in the past.

One should not think that one stays only in a single level of consciousness, although it may dominate for days or weeks or years at a time. One may experience all the levels in a day, or even in an hour. And it is helpful to remember when these painful levels are experienced, that they will change. Most of the time, however, we see whatever space we are in as Reality, and can't remember that there is anything else.

It gets worse before it gets better, as you can see from the chart, because the next level is psychic panic and suicide, "the dark night of the soul." For me it is a feeling of panic so strong that my body and psyche feel as though they would split apart. I am terrified. My mind haunts me with images of disaster, personal and social, which paralyze me and make me barely able to take care of myself and my children. I want *out,* although I am afraid to commit suicide I have continual fantasies of escaping my life. It is a state in which being inside the body and psyche is intolerable. Some people actually kill themselves, of course. Most of us stop short, but quit jobs, leave marriages, abuse drugs and alcohol, move out of town, and exhibit other sorts of "getting out of here" behavior.

So therefore, it appears that if you take up any of these paths of meditation, that you will experience several years (or so it has been for me) of sheer hell, in which you will comtemplate suicide many times, have many calamities befall you, and in which no one except a person who understands this process will be able to help:

a private world of despair, madness, and avoidance of "reality" because it is so untenable. I have felt like Job. Although I did not lose my children, I lost everything else. Several times. A never ending saga of tragedy, failure, and bankruptcy. I include this chapter so that you may be forewarned.

Here is an interesting example of how the addition and subtraction of energy works. If you are in one of these uncomfortable states, or if you attempt suicide, you will be given tranquilizers, which lower the level of energy in your system, and bring your psyche back down to a more comfortable level, like the theoretician, or the jet setter, or the good employee.

From the standpoint of handling one's own movement through these states, it may often be easier and preferable to lower the level of energy in the body by various means (selective use of drugs and alcohol, sex with orgasm, overwork, illness) than to try to raise it through meditation. At least one has the choice to continue the meditation or give oneself a little slack. One must be very careful of drug and alcohol abuse, however.

It helps to develop a "hang in there" attitude and to use the Levels of Consciousness map. One must learn to tolerate and manage the uncomfortable states until they lift. As more and more people begin to have these experiences we will have to develop a class of counselors who understand the process and can help, rather than dishing out drugs or locking people up.

Chapter Ten

Sex Therapy

I had the good fortune to work for almost a year in a sex therapy clinic, and learned a great deal about sexual dysfunctions and their treatment. I can say at this time, with certainty, that there is no reason for any American to suffer from any sexual dysfunction any longer. More than ten years ago, Masters and Johnson developed the techniques that therapists use today, and they are eighty percent effective. My opinion is that the other twenty percent do not follow instructions.

Most sexual dysfunctions are caused by the abysmal ignorance we have of our own bodies and our sexual functioning. Most cures involve masturbation.

In the case of women, the most common dysfunction is not being able to have orgasm. There is one and only one cause: women do not know their own bodies, are reluctant to touch their own bodies and find out what turns them on and gives them orgasm.

When I was a pre-orgasmic woman I thought there was something deeply wrong with me psychologically because I never came. Then I learned how to do it and dropped that theory.

Many women also have such a low level of vitality that they have hardly enough *energy* in their bodies to produce orgasm. They need to take up sports and exercise that involves the legs (jogging, tennis) because this stimulates the vital energy of the body. It is well known that physical activity stimulates sexuality. Joggers have better sex than their sedentary friends!

The most common male dysfunctions are premature ejaculation and impotence.

In my observation, eighty percent of impotence is relational, that is, men don't know that it won't go up for a lady they don't like or one who has been screaming at them for thirty years. Some men put a woman on a pedestal, making themselves inferior, and therefore lose their virility. All these men find out very quickly, when playing with a new companion, that there is nothing "wrong" with them at all.

The other twenty percent is caused by lack of vitality. Middle aged men, who have been sitting at desks all their lives, smoking, drinking alcohol, and literally allowing their bodies to go to pot, lose their erective capacity. Erection, after all, is a mechanical problem of circulation. If your physical condition and your circulation are poor, erections will be poor. A man in good health, with a partner he likes or loves, will live a long and happy life with no erective failure as long as he lives.

There are also a few men who are impotent because of deep-seated fear or hatred of women, but the number is too small to be concerned with.

Premature ejaculation is particularly insidious. In my opinion, there can be no deep sexual satisfaction with a couple if they are unable to have extended periods of penile-vaginal contact. This has nothing whatsoever to do with the ability to have orgasm, because most women do not have orgasms by penetration alone. So men should learn to stay hard *not* because it will make their women come, but because it will create a deep sense of contact and communication which can be achieved no other way.

Men who have a problem of premature ejaculation are likely to become impotent in later years. In my opinion this is because sex is never deeply satisfying to themselves and their partners, and simply dies out, as the vitality lessens and the relationship dies out.

If you are interested in techniques to relieve sexual dysfunctions, in addition to simply using my masturbation exercise, read *Understanding Human Sexual Inadequacy,* the Masters and Johnson-authorized explanation of their work, by Fred Belliveau and Lin Richter, (Little, Brown and Company, Boston, 1970). *Male Sexuality* by Bernie Zilbergeld is also very valuable. (Little, Brown and Company, Boston, 1978).

The basic technique in training for ejaculatory control is to teach oneself to stop short of orgasm. The best way to begin this is in making love to oneself. That's why some of my students learned ejaculatory control while doing my exercise, although that was not their purpose at the outset.

Another thing people don't seem to understand is that one must be in a relaxed state in order to experience arousal and sexual pleasure. The nerves which control the sexual responses are shut down by muscular and psychic tension.

The first session with each of my clients at the clinic was a session of nothing but relaxation, cuddling, and breathing together. A whole hour of simple physical contact and touching. Most people make love late at night when they are physically exhausted and uptight. They jump into bed, diddle a little here and there, screw for two and a half minutes (the national average, says Masters and Johnson) after which the man comes and the woman doesn't, and they both fall asleep.

I recommend to couples who are having trouble with their sex lives, that they spend as much time as possible lying around together, holding each other, cuddling, breathing in unison together, and touching each other in non-sexual ways. I also recommend that they masturbate, that they have a sex life with themselves as well as with their sexual partners, so they can develop their erotic nature and learn what gives them pleasure. I have no patience with couples who blame each other for their failures, or who refuse to masturbate because "it's so much better with a partner."

They also have to learn to communicate. That means talk about what they like and don't like sexually, discuss their ideas for creative sex, their fears and concerns. *It is time to stop claiming that the other person is somehow supposed to just know what to do for us, and when, in order to give us the maximum sexual experience.* Everyone must be responsible for their own sexuality and their own orgasms. Women are particularly guilty of this attitude, laying the blame on their partners for not being some sort of magician or Valentino, when they themselves do not know what it takes for them to have a satisfactory sexual experience.

In addition, sex doesn't work if one partner is always active—always doing the touching and stimulating. Most often the active partner is the man, with the result that he doesn't get proper stimulation himself, and his partner is denied the joy of being active. It is important to be Androgynous in our sexual behavior: active sometimes, receptive sometimes.

The responsibility for your sexual problems is your own, not your partner's. As long as you are a repressed, asexual person, you will attract other repressed, asexual people as your partners. Turn yourself on, develop your own eroticism, and you will find, and attract, partners like yourself.

Pay attention to your attitude toward pleasure. The more pleasure you allow yourself in your life experience, the more your erotic potential will develop. Repression starts with denial of the value and importance of pleasure. All work and no play makes Jack not only a dull boy, but a Eunuch.

Another fault in our modern sexual experience is that we ignore completely the non-physical aspects of sex. We think that turning someone on means pressing the right buttons that we learned in our sex manuals. We ignore completely the turn-on value of conversation, eye contact, flirtation, and Romance in all its dimensions.

Finally, give up the idea that sex equals orgasm. It is the most destructive idea we have. Orgasm is part of the sexual experience, for sure, but less than five percent of it, in my opinion. The rest, and by far the most important, is play, touching, cuddling, loving, and intense stimulation short of orgasm. If one cannot have orgasms, or course, one should learn. But once it is learned, orgasm should assume its proper place in the total sensual/sexual experience: a minor one.

I repeat: there is no reason for anyone to suffer from a sexual dysfunction. If my exercise alone doesn't help you, find a reputable Sex Therapist.

Chapter Eleven

The Sexual Education
Of Children

One of the greatest injustices we do to our children is to systematically, if unintentionally, cut them off from their sexuality. We teach them with the intensity of our full parental power that sex doesn't exist, or shouldn't exist, and we do this most effectively by teaching them not to masturbate. If children were allowed to discover their bodies by themselves there would be no need for Masters and Johnson—there would be no sexually dysfunctional individuals.

Once we teach them not to masturbate it is easy to teach them not to feel their sexual energy in their bodies and not to approach others in a physical way. And since we as parents are not sexual beings and do not relate to our children in a physical way after they are infants, this means that our children grow up with very little physical touching. Is there anyone who still doesn't recognize the need of human beings for touch? How many workshops have I attended in which adults broke into tears when they received the first loving touch they'd had in twenty, thirty, forty years?

Human beings need to integrate their sexuality and they need to be touched. Children are little human beings and they need to be touched too! They need to be stroked, held, cuddled, slept with, until they are able to find others in the outside world, outside the family, to relate to physically and emotionally.

So let's examine our fears about changing our child-rearing practices in this way. In the first place we are all afraid that if our children are allowed to explore and experience their sexuality that social disaster will befall them in the world outside the family. They will be arrested for molesting little boys or girls in the park, and so on. When my children were pre-school age, my husband and I and four other families created a daycare center which we called "The Family Center," which we ran cooperatively for three years, and which grew to twenty families with two professional teachers. We obtained permission from the city of Los Angeles to use an empty park building in our neighborhood, and one day, shortly after moving into our new space, we discovered that our little preschool kiddies were engaging in oral sex in the bathroom.

Nice middle class folks that we were, we were horrified! Hours and hours of discussion followed, full of "what ifs," worries about their futures, and the dangers of shutting off what appeared to be their natural behavior as well as the dangers of letting it continue. We finally decided that we were too confused sexually ourselves to make proper decisions regarding our children's sexuality, and that as long as the sexual behavior stayed within the social circle of the Family Center and caused no problems in the outside world, we would ignore it. We swallowed our fears and waited. At least there was no danger of pregnancy.

And nothing happened. The children's experimentation continued for several months, and then disappeared. When asked why, my five year old responded, "Well, you know when you fuck someone, everyone talks about it." That was the only answer I ever got. Never during that time, or afterwards, did the children attempt to take their experimentation outside of our group; in fact they seemed to *know* even though they were only two to six years old, that the other kids in the neighborhood were somehow not in the game and shouldn't have been. That was our first amazing discovery—that young as they were, they *knew* what was socially appropriate.

This sense of appropriateness has continued; and my children insist that *I* act appropriately also and not embarrass them. They won't even let me belch in public, and my son has a fit if I don't close the bathroom door.

It is important to remember that in our society children legally belong to their parents until they are eighteen. I would never support sex education in the schools, for example, which was not condoned by the children's parents and reflective of *their* best sexual attitudes. But what this small study indicates is that individual parents can allow their children to discover their sexuality. There is a built in knowing in the children which will keep their behavior private and acceptable outside their home or their own social circle.

By *allow* and *discover* I mean just that. Children need very little *teaching* about sex. They are human beings, sexual beings, and they can discover their sexuality and how it works very well by themselves. They can ask their parents or other adult figures when they have questions, and then go back to their own experimentation and discoveries.

Adults for that matter would need very little teaching about sex if they had been able to discover how their sexuality works as children. The very idea that we should need sex manuals is evidence that we have been systematically trained out of our sexuality from an early age.

In addition to our fears of socially inappropriate behavior are our fears of incest. We are afraid that if we were to relate to our children physically, giving them the touching and caressing their bodies and souls need, the energy would turn sexual and incest would result. We also hear about the high rate of incest in families.

I've had a lot of therapy and I've done a lot of work on the Oedipal questions. I've made love to my father and my mother *in fantasy* and found it tremendously exciting and liberating. Exciting because it is a tremendous turn-on, and liberating because those fantasies somehow left me freer; more able to relax and relate to my real sexual partners. But I am convinced that real parents and children want most of all to love each other, to relate to each other from the heart. I have never been interested in being sexual with my children, and the more I learn to relate to them from my heart—the more I learn to love them—the more I am convinced that although our relationship will be physical, it will not be sexual. My function in my relationship with my children is to love them and thereby give them the capacity to love others. It has nothing to do with sex. My suspicion is that actual incest would disappear if we as a society had integrated and accepted and satisfied our sexual needs. In fact, most of the cases of incest are in families in which the parents are not satisfied in their sexual relations with each other and try to get their sexual needs satisfied with the child as a substitute. If they knew how to make love to themselves, they would not be so in need of a substitute.

To begin to heal this fear of incest in yourself, start by relating to your children from your heart. That means putting your *attention* in your heart and waiting to see what your impulses will be. As you can imagine, it takes time. It means you will not come to a child with preconceived ideas about how your play together will proceed. You will put yourself in a child's presence, put your attention in your heart, and follow your impulses. Your arms and hands are connected to your heart and are the instruments for carrying out your impulses. So as you hang out with your child and pay attention to your heart and follow your impulses, you will probably touch the child, and it will be the kind of touching he/she needs—touching from the heart. Love.

Kids need to explore their sexuality and they need to touch and be touched. For hundreds of years our society has done very poorly in giving our children these things they need.

Chapter Twelve

Sex and Being Overweight

I am not the first to suggest that food is a substitute for love. I am also convinced that there is a relationship between overweight and an unwillingness on the part of the fat person to be a sexual being. In our society fat is considered to be sexually unattractive. If one considers sex to be bad, and wants to take oneself out of the game, an easy way to do it is to get fat.

I was twenty pounds overweight from just before puberty until last year. It's interesting that the fat came on just when I was developing that sexual energy which might have been attractive to other sexual beings. I was miserable in high school because I never had any dates and wasn't invited to the senior prom, and in college also had few dates and few boyfriends. I believed that men didn't like me because I was fat, and tried diet after diet with no success. I was five foot eight and 140 pounds from about age sixteen on.

Now you might say that isn't fat, it's just a Rubens style of body; but the Rubens style has been out of fashion for quite a number of years, and that's still enough weight to take one out of the dating game. In recent years I worked on the idea that in spite of my weight I could attract men who *liked* my style of body, and since that time I haven't had a man tell me I'm fat, even though in the last few years I gained another twenty pounds. I also put pictures of Rubens types on the walls in my bedroom to try to accept my body and appreciate it as it is, since I never had any success at losing weight. But after two years of trying to love myself as a Rubens, I had to admit that I, like most others, prefer a Playboy style of body and wanted to have mine as close to that style as it can be.

In recent years I gave up dieting altogether and subscribed to the idea that I could "think thin." The theory is that the mind controls everything, even what happens to food after it enters the body, and that one can therefore eat anything one likes as long as one thinks that it won't go to fat. The only difference between fat people and thin people, according to the theory, is that thin people think, "No matter what I eat, I can't gain weight," and fat people think, "No matter what I eat, it goes directly to fat." Change your thoughts and you can change your body.

So for four years I ate anything I wanted and gained five pounds a year. A year ago, at 160 pounds, and calculating that by 1987 I would weigh 200, I decided that either the theory wasn't true, or, it wasn't working for me.

Nonetheless, eating whatever I wanted to was a very healing process. My relationship to food had been one of torture and denial ever since infancy. I recalled that as an infant, my mother had me on a four hour schedule for feeding, and it didn't suit my nature at all. I could have eaten a little every hour or two and been happy. Even today I am a nibbler, and I love Chinese restaurants because you can order a lot of things to taste and take the rest home. So my relationship to food was and still is, a matter of gulping and inhaling my food—eating fast and too much for fear that there won't be anymore for a long time.

The other advantage of eating whatever I wanted for four years was that my internal child loved it. Since I was fat almost all my life, I was told that I couldn't have any of those fattening things—potato chips, candy bars, and the like; and whenever I *did* have them, I couldn't enjoy them because of course I felt guilty. Being given the idea that I could eat whatever I wanted, I found that I didn't really want certain things, potato chips for example, and that I could innocently enjoy some of my other loves, like french fries. Enjoyment and pleasure returned to the act of eating, since there was no longer a feeling of guilt. My little kid inside could have whatever she wanted and enjoy it, and I think that period of years has helped her to grow up. Now, as I am limiting my food intake, she is willing for that to happen and will not sabotage me.

During this period I also noticed that many of the commonly held truths and rules about food are not valid. I was in the best health I have enjoyed in my life, even though I was taking in many forbidden foods, and I began to notice how many contradictory theories of diet are preached these days, each claiming to possess the secret of health and explaining away their own illnesses.

During this same four year period I was also investigating and healing my relationship to sexual energy, and teaching my Sexual Energy Seminar. I came to the realization that sex is not only *not* bad and *not* dirty, it is a path to experiences of the divine. I began to feel like a sexual person instead of a dead person, and became, in the last six months before this writing, very dissatisfied with my body, not only because I prefer another shape to look at, but because the new, sensuous lady inside me needed a new costume. I couldn't play the role of a sexy lady in the costume of a dowdy housewife.

However, nothing changed my weight for a long time. In August, realizing that the *eat what you like* system wasn't working for me, I gave up sugar almost entirely. The following spring, as I was having trouble with my colon, I started substituting raw vegetables for one meal a day, and thought that that *must* influence my body to drop some weight. In June I made it a goal that I would lose ten pounds by Labor Day and another ten pounds by Christmas. By July, almost a year after giving up sugar, nothing had happened. I was very discouraged, but still very determined. While in Milwaukee to do my workshop, I decided to give up alcohol and go on a fast. My favorite drinks were Amaretto, Galliano, and Kahlua, and I realized that I might be *drinking* a candy bar a day. I switched to Perrier and Virgin Marys with lots of Tabasco.

In the past, the very idea of fasting would make me crazy. I tried it several times, and never got past two o'clock in the afternoon of the first day, because by that time I would be flat on my back and unable to move from lack of energy. I would have to cancel all my appointments for the rest of the day, and the idea of being weak and unable to work for the duration of the fast would always make me give up.

However, this time I was determined. I felt that it was necessary to let my body know I meant business when I said I was going to lose weight. I had a week in San Diego, at home, between the trip to Milwaukee and a trip to Montreal, and I decided that I would fast for four days and come off the fast gently the last three days, because I didn't want to be fasting in the presence of all those croissants and great restaurants in Montreal. So, after a delicious lunch at my favorite pizza parlor, I began a fast of mineral water and herb teas.

On the second day I had a headache, which I cured with soporific teas like chamomile and scullcap, and on the third day I was quite nauseous, so I drank some bouillon. I also added carrot juice to the fast on the third day because I was feeling weak and wanted to correct that. Contrary to my expectations, the worst thing I could say about the fast was that I was bored. The hunger didn't bother me, I continued my usual hectic schedule, and realized that my body can do very well with a fraction of the food I put in it. I felt extremely proud of myself for having accomplished such a miracle and began believing that I had broken my addiction to food. A month later I was still eating about half what I usually ate, with no sugar or alcohol.

Three weeks after the fast I weighed myself and had lost nine pounds. By Labor Day I had lost eleven pounds and felt confident for the first time in my life that I could lose that twenty pounds. It was gone by Thanksgiving. During the holidays I relaxed my eating habits and enjoyed the available goodies, gaining five pounds back, which I lost in January, quite easily.

How did this happen? My belief is that since I discovered the relationship between sex and weight, and was able to clean up my negative ideas about sex, I was able to *feel* that other body I wanted, that sensuous woman. Since I could feel her, and really wanted to be like her, I could listen to her instructions. Perhaps it was she who originally told me to give up sugar and alcohol. It was certainly she who suggested the fast and told me what to do in the rough spots.

How does this differ from the other "think thin" methods which didn't work? Well, if being thin means being sexy, then it's clear that a person would have to be willing to be sexy and feel like she or he could handle that before he or she would be willing to be thin. And secondly, the thin lady doesn't just *think* she can't get fat; she *eats* differently than the fat lady. She drinks Perrier and Virgin Marys. She eats salads. She runs and dances and plays racquetball. She *behaves* differently than the fat lady. And furthermore, it is an internal process, not one imposed from outside. I was never able to follow a diet forced on me by my parents or doctors who said I should lose weight. I was never able to tell *myself* to lose weight. And the idea of a thin lady, a sensuous lady, inside me who could direct the process, was very important.

As my expanded sexuality changed into a philosophy of self love, I also stopped trying to get love by eating. I was able to give it to myself, from inside.

There is one more remark I would like to make about the thin lady. She is not a mother. Nancy Friday, in her book *My Mother, Myself,* points out that mothers, by their nature, are opposed to sex. Even the archetype of Mother, Demeter, is not into sex. She refuses even such dashing lovers as Poseidon, and is so enraged when her daughter Persephone runs off to make it with the god of the underworld, that she forbids the crops to grow.

According to Nancy Friday, when a woman becomes a mother, she gives up her sexuality, trades it in, in favor of mothering. In my process of becoming a sensuous, thinner woman, I realized early on that I would have to ask the mother in me to move over. That is not to say that I do not have feelings and gestures of mothering towards my children and my lovers, but rather to say that those feelings, that way of being, manifests only in relation to them. It is not my presentation of myself twenty-four hours a day.

This is one of the most exciting things that has ever happened to me, as exciting as the first time I learned to give myself an orgasm. I feel like an alcoholic who has kicked the habit, or a cigarette smoker who has successfully given up smoking; the exquisite triumph of doing something I believed I could not do. I am also exercising, doing yoga, calesthenics, T'ai Chi and Kung Fu—acivities I had previously scorned because they took too much effort and made me tired. It's not that I can do these things because I've lost weight, but because there is a new being expressing herself through me.

Taking charge of one's own body, one's sexuality, and one's need for love is the best way to tackle a weight problem. It also gives one the strength to maintain a diet when surrounded, as we are by delicious things to eat.

Chapter Thirteen

Sex and Aging

In China, old people are looked upon with reverence and respect. In our culture, old people are looked upon as an inconvenience.

In China, old people's sex lives are as strong as the young, and they are considered desirable partners for men and women in their twenties and younger. In our culture older people are considered not only undesirable sexual partners and companions, it is commonly believed that they aren't sexual beings at all, or at least have a hard time performing.

Old Chinese people look relaxed, serene, and satisfied with their lives. Our old people look scared, uptight, and unhappy. Perhaps we have something to learn from the Chinese.

In the last few years I have dated a couple of older men, that is, men twenty or twenty-five years older than I, and was astonished at what excellent lovers they were, what great companions there, and how many things I enjoyed *because* of their age, not in spite of it.

First of all, an older man has status. When I walk in the room on the arm of the bank president and people turn their heads, giving him that recognition of status and achievement, I am impressed. (The most they'll ever turn their heads at *me* for is my looks). I appreciate being able to bask in that energy second hand, and I hope some day I'll have it for myself. A man in his fifties or older has very likely accomplished a great deal, learned an appreciable amount from experience, and is therefore a companion that no younger man can equal.

There's no reason why the body should lack any vitality or attractiveness in a person over fifty. All my older lovers have been sportsmen with beautiful, excellently functioning bodies. Most of them were in better shape physically than I. That, by the say, is another lesson from the Chinese. Have you ever seen a

T'ai Chi master in his sixties or older? Often you can't tell how old he is, because he looks so young, and his body is in excellent physical shape. The truth is simple: if you take care of your body it will serve you willingly and with strength and agility for your whole life.

Masters and Johnson say that age should bring no decline or failure in sexual functioning. Perhaps since we believe that sex is bad anyway, and we let our bodies get out of shape, the sexual function dies before the body. With sex, as with everything else, one should keep in shape and keep in practice. See the chapter on Sex Therapy for my comments about aging and impotence.

I once had an older lover who couldn't perform on our first encounter, but I found that love, patience, and an attitude of playfullness cured him very quickly. His body was already in good shape.

There are a number of ways in which an older man or woman is definitely a better lover than a younger person. Through experience they have learned control of their own sexual energy so they can stay with you for a long time. And through experience, if they have allowed themselves to be sexual beings, they have learned the delights of the body and can teach them to the younger partner.

In *The Tao of Love and Sex,* Jolan Chang says that in ancient China it was very common for older women to be with very young men and older men to be with very young women. There were some specific reasons. One is that an older woman's vagina might be less tight and therefore a young man could more easily learn control. And for an older man, the tighter vagina of a young girl would provide more stimulation. The other reasons were the value of older people as teachers (there's no more certain recipe for sexual disaster than two virgins) and the fact that the combination of ''parent'' and sexual partner is a definite turn-on.

We all have sexual fantasies about our parents. The most talked about fantasies are the young boy's about his mother and the young girl's about her father. I am convinced that we fantasize about both parents with equal excitement, if we give ourselves permission to do so. Many therapists nowadays recommend fantasizing having sex with our parents in order to heal our hangups about sex and make us more free to experience the kind of sex lives we want.   And it is an even greater experience to act out the fantasies with a person who is old enough to be our parent. The first time I discovered this was by accident. A man twenty years older and I were making love, and he suggested that we pretend that I was his daughter, and he would call me by his daughter's name. Well, the scene was remarkable—I turned into a little thirteen-year-old Lolita getting off on her father like crazy. It was one of the most remarkable sexual experiences I've ever had.   Since then I've devised several other "Daddy" games to play with equal delight.

More than the sex games of parent and child, is another level of relating with older lovers which is marvelously satisfying and cannot be done with younger partners. When an older lover is holding me tenderly, I feel like I'm being held by my father, the way I always wanted him to hold me. When I'm held in this way, the hurt little girl in me is healed, and is able to grow up. It also extends to our activities together. Sometimes when we go somewhere together I feel like I'm on an outing with my Daddy—that he has taken me somewhere because he really wants to be with me, and I get to have another experience that my internal child loves.   It's great therapy and extremely satisfying.

The Chinese say that not only are older people as sexually active as younger people, but love, sexual love, is one of the keys to longevity, along with good food and exercise. It would be interesting to see if introducing sex to old people in this country would smooth out the aging process and make people live longer. It would certainly make old age more fun.

Jolan Chang, himself over sixty, says he always makes love several times a day. "Often on a Sunday I make love two or three times in the morning and then go cycling for nearly the whole day, about twenty or thirty miles, and then make love again before going to sleep. The result is that I am not in the least exhausted, and my health could not be better or my mind more tranquil."

I'm forty, and I spend a lot of time thinking about what I'd like to do with the second half of my life. My belief and my intention is that my sex life will get better and better as I get older. My friends say I already look much younger than my actual age. I will be curious to see if the sexual technique I practice, combined with diet and exercise will keep me looking and feeling young when I am sixty.

Chapter Fourteen

Dracula

Dracula is a name that has for centuries (according to the producers of the Frank Langella movie) provoked terror in the hearts of men and passion in the drawers of women. The new movie was billed as "A Love Story" and I was delighted, because ever since I first saw a version of the story many years ago, I have known that it was not only about love, but about sex, about passion, and about our fascination and fears about sex and passion.

Here's Count Dracula, everyone's perfect Prince Charming—perfectly beautiful, perfectly charming, perfectly attractive, and irresistibly seductive. He is Mr. Sex. He dresses in a dashing manner, comes from a very old aristocratic family, lives in a fairyland mansion—a dream lover of the first dimension for anyone. He is passionate, considerate, intense, devoted, and in this movie anyway, a fantastic lover. The love scene between him and Lucy is photographed in a flaming red spiralling mist that shows they are experiencing the heights of cosmic sex. There's no doubt that whatever happens, the experience is definitely worth it. After being with him even once, his lovers are devoted to him forever and will cross even the barrier of death to be with him and continue the good stuff. Who could ask for more?

And yet the Count is a villain, and the heroes put every ounce of their energy and the wisdom of the ages and the Christian Church into killing him.

This movie is a delightful and perfect example of out society's attitudes towards passion and sex. Sex is evil and dangerous—it could get you killed. Stay away from it, cut it out of your heart and your body.

The first victim saves the Count from death at the beginning of the movie. She is irresistibly drawn from her bed in the middle of the night in the pouring rain to a cave where he has apparently crawled after a shipwreck.

The scene where they connect for the first time is priceless. He is lying under a delicious looking fur rug and all one can see is his hand. She extends her hand to his, passionately, innocently, because she has no idea what she is doing there, and he takes her hand—first with the first two fingers in a sinister, claw-like fashion, and then with the rest of his hand, in the most loving, fatherly, tender gesture imaginable. One falls in love even with his hand. And from the beginning the image is clear—passionate love is somehow evil, in contradiction to human life.

I have been amazed, in my life and work, how many people are afraid of passion. It's true, you can get hooked on it. It's true, you suffer if you lose the one you're passionate about. But to me, *a life without passion is a life without blood,* contrary to the presentation of the movie and our prevailing social views. In the movie, of course, those who are seduced into that passionate space lose their blood and their lives. Dracula needs other people's blood to keep his own life going, and he prefers women.

One of the problems with passionate involvements is that we may lose our identity (our souls, if you will) in the process. "Thou shalt have no other gods before me" means, among other things, that there is always something higher than the relationship—the individual's spiritual process, the individual's creative work, the individual's sense of centering and growth. Everyone has been in or has observed relationships in which one partner has become lost in the other. It doesn't work.

But the other "dangers" of sex and passion are largely socially taught and can be eliminated from consciousness and literature. In the beginning of the movie there are darkness, storms, and spooky music to set the scene for evil and fear. I have investigated the evil of sex and I find that in this case, evil is what our parents and our society have taught us is evil. There is no spook about to get us if we develop and encourage our sexual nature and our passion. Our deep fears about our sexuality are not connected to some reality in nature, they are taught to us at our parents' knees and have been taught that way for countless generations. It doesn't matter why the process got started, but my guess is that sexless people are easier to control—the eunuchs were the best example. Take away a person's sex and he is magically your servant. Not only is he sexless, but mindless as well; without will.

The hero in the story is the father of the first victim. He is the patriarch, grey and creaky, who comes to investigate his daughter's death and then sets out to destroy the Count. One of the negative aspects of the patriarch, the macho energy of the universe, is the effort to control.

It is also our parents, our mothers as well as our fathers—who have trained us out of our sexuality, with violence if necessary. (''If you touch that thing one more time I'm going to cut it off.'')

The father does get some help from a younger man, the lover of the second victim, but it is *he* who has all the knowledge about how to fight vampires. It is also he who, with his dying breath, hurls the weapon which catches the Count. This enables the younger man to hoist him up into the sunlight to his gruesome demise.

The other weapons used against the Count are silver crosses and communion wafers (the church, of course is opposed to sex) and garlic. I don't know the reason for the garlic, but I guess for most people, as for the Count, the smell of too much garlic would make one un-kissable. There is a great little incest scene in which the old man's daughter, now a vampire, goes for her father with a great, lustful, ''Come with me, Papa,'' and he stops her with his garlic breath and his silver cross. The Count himself is associated with bats, wolves, spiders, night, coffins, blood, and death—about the most negative symbols our society can muster. Sunlight kills him. Of course for many years, most sexual activity has taken place at night, in bed, under the sheets, and full of guilt. It is only recently that our sexuality has been coming out into the sunlight, in thought and in practice, and guess what? In the sunlight it doesn't look horrible and die at all; it is enhanced and enriched. Another myth destroyed.

There is a lot of male chauvinism in the picture too. Lucy, the second victim, has been smitten, or rather bitten, with passion for the Count, and is willing to do anything to be with him and keep their thing going. Having been given blood transfusions from her first lover, she jumps out of bed and races towards the count's castle in a small carriage. The men, however, follow her in a car (men always have superior weapons and everyone knows they are swifter and more powerful than women) and they catch her, wrestle her to the ground, and lock her up in a mental institution which is conveniently run by her own father. *Her* father wants to keep her from sex as badly as the first victim's father. However, her man (Dracula) is more powerful than all the fathers and the lover combined, and comes to save her (women always need to be saved).

Dracula promises Lucy life on a higher plane, and she believes him, since she has already experienced the highest states she ever dreamed possible on *this* plane, and she's ready to go the next step. He even promises that they will create a Utopian society together. ("We will create more of our kind.")

In the end, even though she has been overpowered by the men again, has had her Count torn from her side, and will no doubt resume a normal, dull life with her old lover, as she watches the Count's soul fly from his body, she smiles a smile of recognition and pleasure. There are no words, but it looks like she is saying, "I may have lost him, but at least I've known love. I'll remember him for the rest of my life." This movie says, "If you allow yourself to be a passionate person it will get you into trouble."

The standard way to kill a vampire is to drive a stake through his heart. The best way to kill passion is to separate the heart from the genitals, to separate sex from love, and our society has done this most effectively. The phenomenon is sometimes called the "Madonna/ Whore Complex" and means that the person you love you can't fuck and the person you fuck, you don't love. What I am teaching in my workshops is a method of connecting the heart to our sexuality; in fact, a method of using the sexuality to open the heart.

It is interesting that in this new movie the stake-in-the-heart routine doesn't work because Dracula is too powerful and too smart, and he has to be stabbed in the back, hooked by a meathook, and hoisted into the sunlight in order to do him in. Indeed, in our society, it is becoming less and less possible to teach people that sex is bad and to be avoided. The sexual revolution has taken place. What remains is to connect the genitals to the heart; to bring sex and love together. The father of the first victim cuts the heart out of his dead daughter's body in order to break her connection to the count. We must put the heart back into our sexuality to experience the passionate relationships we know we deserve.

The heart is also a safety valve. When the heart is open, when love is flowing, the possible evils of a strong sexual drive are eliminated because the heart wishes no one ill. It knows what other people need, it listens, it wishes them only good. It is stronger than the sexual drive and directs it towards the highest good.

Chapter Fifteen

Conclusion

It's been a hard winter, in fact, three hard winters. Deep depression, paralysis of my creative powers, financial crisis, very poor health. This year was the worst.

Yesterday, feeling alive for the first time in many weeks, I gave myself a full body massage. As I worked away at my body, which was recovering from an illness, I thought about how the Mongolian Warriors used to do a deep self-massage after every battle, to get the fear out of the body so the warrior would be fresh, innocent, for the next battle.

There will no doubt be another battle. But now there is a feeling of rebirth, as if coming back from death. My psyche seems to have seasons. There are times when everything is dark and wintry, cold and dead. It has been this way all my life. I had hoped that the way I have been using my sexual energy would change this pattern, but it has not.

Even in the darkest times I make love to myself almost every day. Sometimes it lifts me completely out of the darkness and into the light for a few hours; a welcome relief. Now, as I am coming out of the trough, and feeling reborn, I discover again the joy of the body, the electric feeling in muscles and joints, the need to stretch, and stretch.

What a long road I have come with this body! How long it has taken for me to want to take care of it and love it. How many years of bad food, pollutants, and slovenliness I now must heal.

Most certainly one of the results of my program of self love is that I have come to love my body. I had to lose weight to do it, and I am still working with all my might on exercise and diet improvements. But I have a respect and a love and appreciation of this body that I did not have before. I have a sense of myself as being not my body, but inseparable from it.

Last week I took a day off and went to the country. I started my day with a good soak in a hot mineral bath, and ended it with a many course dinner in a gourmet restaurant, also in the country.

In the hot spring were a number of couples (no one alone) who had also come to enjoy the healing waters. They were in their fifties and sixties: fat, stiff, pasty looking, and sexless. No couple seemed to have a loving connection between them, as they did not touch, or look at each other, and seemed to prefer not to talk or even sit with each other. I imagined that they were stiff, pasty, and fat because, in addition to poor diet and lack of exercise, they had never allowed themselves to be sexual beings. I decided that their relationships had died in the bud because they never connected their hearts and their genitals, never formed a bond of love.

Later in the restaurant I watched the waiters: stiff, shoulders hunched up as if to keep their hands away from their genitals. They looked scared, separated from their bodies, prospective clients for a sex therapist in later years. I could see them, embarrassed, confessing to the therapist, "I'm afraid of women. I don't get hard anymore. I come too fast. My wife isn't affectionate."

The head waiter at the end of the meal brought me a cup of tea on a huge silver platter with a complete silver service. I imagined giving him a little speech in which I told him that he would feel much better and be a lot happier in life if he would learn to make love to himself. In my fantasy, upon hearing my words, he stiffens with shock and drops the silver platter and all its contents on the starched linen tablecloth.

We are not an erotic society, no matter how many half-clothed women are displayed on billboards, no matter how many fortunes are made on sex magazines. It is still true that scarcely any major director (exceptions: Vadim and Polanski) will consider doing erotic films, nor will competant actors and actresses allow themselves to be photographed in heightened sexual states. Masters and Johnson reported ten years ago that the national average time that a man and woman experience penetration is two and one half minutes. My experience is that sexual ecstasy takes a lot longer than that, and that penetration is an important part of the experience.

The secret of opening your erotic nature is to make love to yourself. If you do, you will find yourself more attractive, more sexual, and have an easier and more satisfying sex life with your partners. Very likely you will be able to heal any sexual dysfunctions you may have. If you learn to make love to yourself you will be more relaxed, more secure within yourself, and less likely to put up with a bad relationship just because it gives you sex or companionship.

If you elect to use your erotic energy to bombard your heart, you will most likely experience other benefits: you will become more loving of yourself, your children, the others in your life. Your self love will stimulate you to take care of your body, the temple, the instrument, the house you live in.

Your relationships will improve because you will be more loving, less dependent, and less demanding. You will have the possibility of creating a pleasure bond, so that when you fall out of love you can fall into loving.

As a culture we are castrated, as surely as though the balls had been cut off every man and the clitoris removed from every woman. Our erotic nature has been forcibly put to sleep. The effects of our castration are seen in more than just our sex lives. Our over concern with material possessions is evidence of our inability to experience love. Our high rate of stress and its accompanying diseases and breakdowns, is related to our inability to experience deeply satisfying sex and love. A great deal of human violence is related to repressed sexuality. Everyone knows they are less angry and less irritable when they are getting loved and laid regularly. I believe that acne and bed wetting could be cured by masturbation. The ravages of old age could be mitigated, in addition to taking better care of the body, by a good sex life. Keep those hormones flowing!

There are only two things to remember: you must first turn yourself on. Then you must raise the sexual energy up in your body—to the heart in the beginning, and then anywhere you wish. This path to ecstasy is natural and simple and available to all human beings. It is like a water faucet that has been shut off so long it has rusted. It may take a bit of an effort at first to turn it on; but the water is there, just waiting to be released.

and Self Love

and Self Love

Design: Douglas Cruickshank